THE COMPLETE GUIDE TO
BEAD JEWELLERY
AND DECORATION

THE COMPLETE GUIDE TO
BEAD JEWELLERY AND DECORATION

**Eagle
Editions**

AN OCEANA BOOK

Published by Eagle Editions Ltd
11 Heathfield
Royston
Hertfordshire SG8 5BW

Copyright © 2006 by Quantum Publishing Ltd
This edition printed 2006

ISBN 1-84573-153-0
QUMCGT3

This book is produced by
Quantum Publishing Ltd
6 Blundell Street
London N7 9BH

Manufactured in Singapore by
Pica Digital Pte. Ltd

Printed in Singapore by
Star Standard Industries Pte. Ltd

CONTENTS

INTRODUCTION

Beads have been used around the world for almost as long as Man has had the means to bore holes and to string the pieces together. Although the earliest beads were made from pieces of animal bone or horn, from shells or from seeds, it was not long before wood, pottery, metals and glass were being used.

The Egyptians wore magnificent jewels, both men and women wearing broad collars made from beads strung in many rows, and Tutankhamen was buried in a ceremonial apron made of gold plates inlaid with multi-coloured glass and threaded with bead borders. Beads were made in China during the Bronze Age, and the Romans used glass to make beads. Etruscan tombs have revealed necklaces, brooches, bracelets and rings, and archaeological finds from Syria have included pottery beads dating from the 5th-10th centuries.

Today, beads are still made all over the world. Go into almost any craft shop or the haberdashery department of a large store and you will find hundreds of different kinds, shapes and colours of bead made from wood, glass, semi-precious stones, coral, metal, pottery and, of course, plastic, which will have been treated in so many ways that it is almost unrecognisable.

TYPES OF BEADS

Glass

Glass is perhaps the most versatile medium for beads. Many of the projects in this book use the little glass beads known as rocailles and bugles. These are available in dozens of colours and a variety of sizes – the smallest ones are often used for embroidery while the larger ones can be used as spacer beads. Opaque rocailles are ideal for loom-work and woven projects, and they can be used to recreate native American patterns. Rocailles and bugles can be transparent, iridescent or opaline. Some are silver lined, which makes them reflect light, others have metallic or pearl finishes. They used to be sold by weight, and they are still sometimes sold in long strings. Today, however, you are more likely to find them in small packets.

At the other end of the scale from the single-colour rocailles and bugles are the wonderfully elaborate millefiori beads. These originated in the Venetian glass works at Murano, where the technique was used to fuse together tiny multi-coloured canes of glass to create the highly patterned beads.

Lampwork beads – that is, beads made from molten glass – are now made all over the world. Millefiori beads are made in India and exported to the West, while in central Europe molten glass is used to cover small pieces of foil or even minute glass flowers to produce exquisite beads. Other lampwork beads are made with two or more colours wound together to create spiral effects, while others contain spirals of fine metal wire. Sometimes two-colour beads are ground so that the underlying colour is revealed.

In the late 19th century, Daniel Swarovski developed a method of refining and cutting glass to create faceted beads and this revolutionised the bead industry. Now many faceted glass beads are made by moulding, and they are, of course,

Plain ceramic beads

Cut crystal beads

Small crystal and glass beads

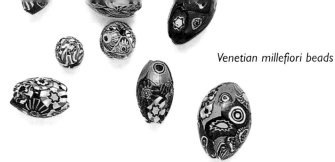

Venetian millefiori beads

much cheaper than hand-cut beads. Nevertheless, they still sparkle and reflect the light, just as the more expensive hand-cut beads do.

Africa has specialised in the production of beads from recycled glass, including old soft-drink bottles, called ground glass beads. These have an opaque finish and are often two- or even three-coloured.

Wood

Wooden beads are among the oldest type to have been made. In Japan and China wooden beads were elaborately carved, often with representational flowers and figures. Elsewhere wood has been simply smoothed and polished so that the natural grain and colour can be appreciated. Yew, holly, oak, walnut and boxwood have all been used in Europe, while hardwood beads, including those made from mahogany, purpleheart and tulipwood, have been made in the Americas.

Metal

Gold and silver beads have been used for millennia to form decorations for kings and princes, and precious metals are, of course, still used today to make beads.

Now, however, you are more likely to see beads made from base metals or even recycled saucepans.

> Africa has specialised
> in the production of beads
> from recycled glass

Although they are not made in sterling silver, but in a silver alloy, beads from the Indian subcontinent are available in a range of traditional shapes and patterns. Filigree beads, which may be made as openwork pieces or with the decoration laid over the solid base, have been made throughout Europe, with the metal wire twisted into abstract and floral motifs in both gold and silver. Hammered metals, especially copper, have been used to create textured surfaces.

As with glass, recycling methods now mean that it is possible to find beads made from old saucepans or even motor parts. These often originate from Africa or the Far East.

Wooden beads

11

Painted ceramic beads

Ceramic

Pottery beads were among the earliest forms of decoration to be made, and today ceramic beads are still made. Plain ceramic beads, such as those made in the UK, are sometimes formed into twisted cones or bicones, and brightly coloured annular beads, dyed with metal oxides, are produced in Greece.

Often, however, ceramic beads are highly glazed and decorated. In Greece there is a tradition of decorating hand-rolled beads with pretty floral motifs, while beads from China will have painted flowers outlined in metallic finishes. Peruvian beads are often decorated with intricately hand-painted scenes and patterns.

some exquisitely simple necklaces. Because these beads tend to be expensive, they are best strung on sturdy thread with a knot between each bead. This helps to prevent the beads from being lost if the thread breaks.

Amber and jet, which are not true stones, can also be used alone or in combination with gold and silver spacers and findings to make traditionally styled pieces. Amber is really the fossilised gum from coniferous trees, and

Semi-Precious Stones

Agate, jade, lapis lazuli, turquoise – the variety of semi-precious stones that can be formed into beads is almost unlimited, and they offer the opportunity to make some lovely pieces. Try alternating semi-precious beads with silver or gold beads to create

Pottery beads were among the earliest forms of decoration to be made

Decorative metal beads

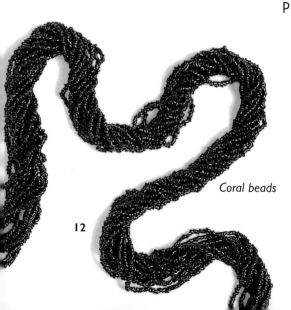

Coral beads

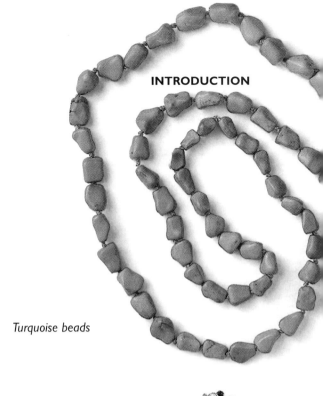

Turquoise beads

its colour ranges from rich red to yellow. Jewellery made from jet, a mineral similar to lignite, has been found in Bronze Age tombs, and it was enormously popular in Britain in the 19th century.

Natural Minerals

Beads from natural materials such as bone, horn (including ivory) and seeds are less likely to be encountered today, unless you find old pieces of jewellery in antique and second-hand shops and decide to give them a new lease of life by restringing them or by reusing the beads in a new way.

Shell beads are still made, however. Mother-of-pearl is sometimes carved into pendants and beads, while both mother-of-pearl and abalone are often inlaid as decoration into plain beads.

Pearls and coral have long been highly valued as beads, and both may be too expensive for everyday use. The wide-scale production of cultured pearls and modern manufacturing methods that have made possible the production of glass imitation pearls and pearlised plastics have brought pearl or pearl-like beads within the reach of all beaders. While these imitations can never emulate the beautiful lustre of real pearls, they offer the beader scope to create some traditional pieces that would otherwise not be possible.

Jet beads

Metal beads

BUYING BEADS

In the introduction we have already mentioned some of the places where you can buy beads, but here we give more details of possible suppliers.

Firstly, there are bead shops. Most big towns have a specialist bead shop, or perhaps a craft supplies shop that sells a selection of beads. This, of course, is where you would have the greatest variety to choose from, and it is very nice to be able to actually see the colours and shapes before you commit yourself. It also gives you the opportunity to try looking at different beads together to see if they really will compliment each other. Some department stores now have a selection of beads in their haberdashery department; if you are keen on doing beadwork or embroidery with rocaille beads this is often a good source.

Secondly, you can buy by mail order, as there are now a host of useful catalogues available, mainly with good colour photography, which makes buying easy. The disadvantage of mail order is the frustration of waiting for your order to come when you have a project ready in your mind, and the acute frustration of items sometimes being out of stock when you have carefully chosen them. This having been said, the bead catalogues are invaluable if you live in a remote area, and they provide a wonderful selection.

What other sources are there? Antique markets will sometimes have damaged necklaces that are better re-made, and the charity shops often have strings of beads that you can re-use with other beads. Ethnic clothes shops usually have some beads that come from the countries that they are dealing with, and market stalls are another possible source. Do not forget to keep an eye out for beads when you are on holiday;

although most countries export their beads to the United States and Europe, it is exciting to find them yourself. Finally, it seems that in some areas people are organising bead parties in their homes, so it is a good idea to be aware of anything like that near you.

Beads are made out of many different materials: ceramics, glass, wood, plastic and bone, and more expensive materials including semi-precious stones such as malachite and lapis lazuli. The list is extensive, and in addition you should remember that there are materials that you can make beads from yourself; polymer clays, paper, air-dried clay and the like.

Most aspects of buying beads are a question of common sense, think of their condition and check from for cracks or rough edges. Think carefully about the size of the holes in relation to the threads that you want to use: nowadays some beads like the Peruvian clay beads are made in the same designs with either large holes for leather or small holes for thread. Think about the types of beads that you are using together; it would be unwise to put very delicate beads between very heavy beads. Be aware of colour fastness: some brightly coloured wooden beads, for example, are susceptible to losing their colour. The content of metal beads needs consideration: some ethnic metal beads are either "white

Do not forget to
keep an eye out for beads
when you are
on holiday

Most beads are
sized in millimetres (mm)
with reference to their
diameter (e.g. 6 mm spheres)
or length times diameter (eg.
15 x 4 mm tubes). The main
exception to this is rocaille beads,
which are the small glass beads, also known
as seed beads, or sometimes pound beads,
which are used for bead weaving, bead
embroidery and with beadlooms. These are
sized by number – usually from 0/11 which
are the smallest to 0/6 which are the largest.
However, the sizing does vary according to
the manufacturer, and can be reversed (i.e.

High-grade silver beads
are likely to be priced by weight
rather than per bead

metal" or low-grade silver, whereas others can
be very high-grade silver and can compare
with sterling silver. If you are using semi-
precious stone beads, or expensive glass
beads, it is sensible to put high-grade silver
with them, if possible. High-grade silver beads
are likely to be priced by weight rather than
per bead, although this is not a strict rule.
There are also many beads available that are
made from metallised plastic; these have a
huge variety of good designs, and seem to be
very durable.

7/0); the basic guide is that the higher numbers are smaller sizes. Other beads often used in bead weaving, embroidery, etc. are bugles; these are small glass tubes, which come in sizes 4 which are the largest, to 1, which is the smallest.

You will quickly learn the sorts of beads that you enjoy working with; some people only work with tiny beads, many others say that they do not have the patience to use small beads but will spend endless hours threading large dramatic beads. Do not forget, as you are hunting for your beads, that older beads represent a lot of history and are very collectable. In the same way, some of the beads that are being made now will be collectable in the future.

MAKING BEADS

A visit to your local crafts store will reveal an array of beads to use in making your jewellery. Be adventurous and use object you can find at home, such as pasta shapes or feathers from a feather duster, to substitute for beads. If you choose to make your own beads, try unusual materials, such as newspaper and magazine cuttings, coloured foil or fabric scraps.

Clay Beads

One of the most effective materials to use is polymer clay. It is available in a fantastic range of colours, moulds easily, and sets hard in a low-temperature oven. There are several comparable brands available, each with their own malleability, baking time, and colour selection.

Plain beads in a single colour can be moulded into any shape you want and then decorated with acrylic paints (water based paints don't cover as well). To make the beads, first knead the clay until it is soft and pliable, then roll it out into a log shape, 0. 5 to 2 cm ($^1/_4$ - $^3/_4$ in) in diameter, depending on how big you want the bead to be. For tube beads, cut the log into equal lengths and pierce the centre with a toothpick or knitting needle. Pierce the bead from both ends to get neat holes; if you just push the stick straight through, make sure that you smooth the rough edges where the stick emerges.

If you choose to make your own beads, try unusual materials

Round beads are made in the same way but each piece of clay is shaped into a ball in the palms of your hands. Pierce holes with a toothpick as above. Square beads are also made from a long log that is then flattened into a square against the edge of a knife or piece of wood. Cut to size and pierce as before. Add texture and detail to plain beads of any shape by pressing modelling tools, coins, and so on, against the surface, or by adding small strips or dots of other colours. Experiment with several colours, for more exciting finishes, such as marbling or millefiori. To create a marbled effect, roll out logs of two or more colours and wrap them around each other. Knead these together, roll them back into a larger log, folding it in half and twisting until the colours are blended. Be careful not to knead too much or the individual colours will disappear and the clay will eventually return to a new, single colour. Shape beads as described above.

Millefiori or "thousand flower" beads are slightly more complicated, but rewarding to make once you have mastered the techniques. Begin with a core colour – either a plain log or two colours rolled together. Then place other logs in different

colours around the core, completely surrounding it. The colours are usually placed in a regular pattern and must be gently pressed together to ensure no air is trapped inside. The whole cane is then wrapped in another sheet of clay, carefully rolled out to a diameter of about 5 mm ($1/4$ in), and cut into tiny slices that are pressed on an unbaked base bead to cover it.

To create a marbled
effect, roll out logs of
two or more colours and wrap
them around each other

Safety Note

Always read the instructions given on the polymer clay package. This clay gives off fumes, especially as it bakes, and should be used in a well-ventilated room.

Fabric Beads

Using paper is one of the easiest and cheapest ways to make beads. The simplest papier-mâchê beads can be made by shaping pieces of newspaper into a ball and then layering pasted strips of newspaper over it. For a smoother finish, layer the paper strips over a ball of plasticine. When the ball is completely dry, cut it in half with a craft knife and remove the plasticine to lighten the paper beads. Glue the two halves of the bead back together and conceal the joint with another layer of paper before decorating.

You can use fabric to make all kinds of beads

To make rolled paper beads, use old wrapping paper or magazines, or paint your own designs onto plain

paper; then cut into strips or elongated triangles, and roll up tightly around a toothpick. To give the finished beads a sheen and a durable finish, paint them with clear nail polish.

Paper Beads

You can use fabric to make all kinds of beads that can be decorated with embroidery or sewn stitches, or even with tiny beads. To make little puffs of fabric, cut the fabric out in circles, hem the edges, and draw up the edges. For tube beads, strips of fabric can be joined and gathered at either end. To give them shape, wrap them over a cardboard base or stuff with a little padding.

Wooden Beads & Pressed Cotton Beads

Most craft suppliers stock unvarnished wooden beads and pressed cotton balls in a variety of sizes. These are both easy to paint and decorate in your own individual style. Support the beads on wooden skewers, tops of pencils, or old paintbrush handles while painting, and leave to dry on a knitting needle stuck in a block of plasticine or polystyrene. Keep patterns simple. If you want to use several colours, let each colour dry before starting the next. When you are finished, protect the surface with a coat of clear varnish or nail polish.

Miscellaneous Bead Ideas

Roll ordinary kitchen foil or coloured candy foil wrappers to make bead shapes. Pierce the centre with a sharp needle and thread into necklaces. Or add coloured foil as a decorative final layer on a papier-mâché bead. Salt dough, which needs to bake in a low-temperature oven for several hours, is another good medium for making beads of different shapes. Both foil and clay can be painted and decorated to suit your design.

Pasta, seeds, nuts, and even washers can be painted, decorated, and strung into spectacular jewellery – no one will ever guess their origins. Use your imagination, and you will discover that all sorts of bits and pieces – safety pins, colourful paper clips, and even rubber bands can be turned into jewellery.

TOOLS & TECHNIQUES

Wire cutters

TOOLS

When you start to work with beads you can manage with very few tools. Scissors and pliers are the main necessity. Pliers are really a question of personal choice. If you are making a lot of straight ear-rings, then a small pair of round-nosed pliers is essential, and it is advisable to use pliers with short "noses" as long ones make your work seem remote. Again, if you are going to do a lot of work with wires, (eyepins, headpins or using jewellery wire), then a pair of wirecutters of snips will make the work easier.

Many of the necklaces in the projects are finished with french crimps or calottes, and you will need pliers to work with these. Once again it is a question of personal taste; flat-nosed pliers are often used but, as you will see from the step by step instructions, we have used sprung round-nosed pliers for this work. Some people find them more awkward, but they are often more powerful – because of this discrepancy the projects refer to necklace pliers, and leave the choice to you.

You will also need a selection of needles, very fine ones if you are working with tiny beads (the long thin beading needles are excellent for loom work, and blunter large-eyed needles will help with larger beads.

Needles

You will need various types of needles for bead work.

1. Fine, pliable beading needles and fine quilting needles are both extremely useful.

2. Leather needles are strong with angled points.

3. Curved needles are invaluable for stitching beads to awkward shapes.

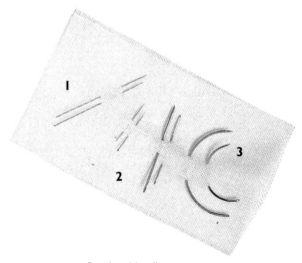

Beading Needles

File, Tweezers & Loom

If you are going to do wirework, then a fine file will be essential. Likewise if you do a lot of knotting or weaving, fine tweezers will be useful. This leads to the subject of looms. The most readily available beadlooms are metal, but they can be quite difficult to use and probably have put many people off this sort of beadwork. If you feel that you will have the patience to work with tiny beads, then it would be advisable to buy a wooden loom, which will make your work very much more enjoyable.

Tweezers

File

Beading Loom

Glues

Your choice of adhesive will depend on the materials you are using. Check the instructions before application.

1. Two-part epoxy glue is very strong and usually dries to a clear finish.

2. A good, general purpose white or yellow craft glue will suffice for most projects.

Glues

Scissors and Bradawl

Scissors

Good scissors are essential for working with beads.

1. Use sharp-pointed embroidery scissors for snipping thread.

2. Use general-purpose craft scissors for other tasks.

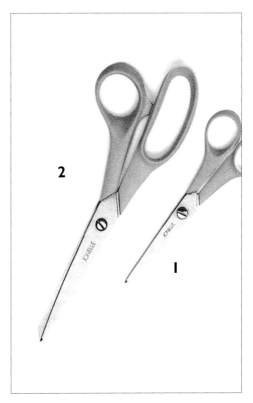

Scissors

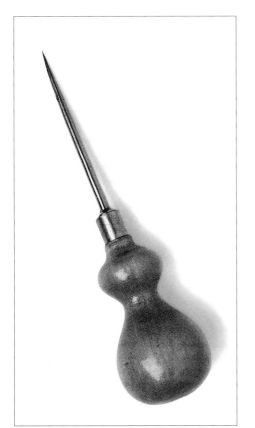

Bradawl

Bradawl

An bradawl or awl is used for starting a hole in leather or hide prior stitching on beads with a needle.

27

Tiger Tail

Threads

You have got your tools and your beads organised, and now it is time to consider what you will put them onto. The easiest threading material is leather, and a few beads with large holes, of course, put onto a thong, with some knots to finish it, can look stunning.

The next material to consider is nylon monofilament (or fishing line, which is basically the same thing). This should be used with caution (some people say that it should never be used!) as it cannot be effectively knotted, so must be used with French crimps or calottes, and it produces stiff results, that do not hang very well. It also has a tendency to shrink, so if you use it, it is advisable to leave a small gap between your beads and fastener to allow for this. The advantage of nylon monofilament is that is has a rigid end for threading, will not fray, and is strong, so it is good for chokers or bracelets that do not need to hang well. It is also a good material for children to work with.

Tiger tail (or soft line) is another good strong threading materials, made of wire with

Leather thonging

a plastic coating. It is excellent for use with heavy beads, but be careful when working with it, as it does not forget any kinks that re made in it, and can snap where it has been kinked. It is best to finish tiger tail with French crimps.

Actual threads are often made of polyester or similar manmade fibres. In this book we have mainly used a thick polyester whipping twine for heavy beads, or a fine polyester thread for small beads. Both of these are very strong and durable, and the thick one comes in several colours and can be supplied with a waxed finish, which makes it possible to use without a needle. This thread is ideal for knotting, plaiting and braiding, and can be used with calottes and French crimps. It hangs nicely and is ideal for most beads, as long as they do not have very small holes. However, if you use it with very heavy beads, it makes sense to allow your necklace to hang

Silk thread

Polyester thread

As well as the threads that we have mentioned, do not forget that there are many beautiful linen threads, exciting cords and, of course, chains to be used. One again, use your imagination, and as you become confident with the techniques, you will be able to use all sorts of materials.

for a few days before you finish the ends, as the thread stretches to a certain extent. The thin polyester is also very strong and is excellent for weaving, loomwork or other use with small beads, and again it can be finished in many different ways.

There are other synthetic threads on the market, all of which can be very useful. Another possibility is silk thread. This is mostly sold on cards, with an integral needle which is extremely helpful. Silk comes in lots of different colours and some different thicknesses, and again is extremely strong and hangs beautifully. The only drawback to it is that it is expensive.

Nylon monofilament

Wire

This can be bought in different gauges, and in different finishes, i.e. silver-plated, brass, etc. Getting used to using wire opens up new horizons in your work. In the book we have shown you how to wire "donuts" and to make your own hooks and jump rings. All good findings suppliers will also supply wire and it makes sense to explore the

Silver wires

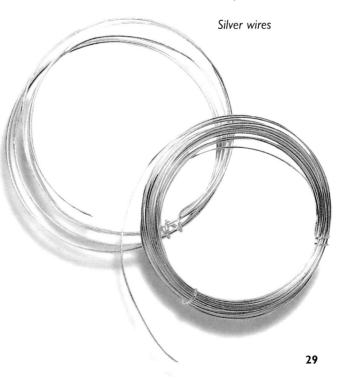

Findings

Findings is the word used to describe the mechanical fittings that are attached to jewellery and that hold the piece on the body or attach it to your clothing. Standard silver findings should always be used when you work with silver. Silver plate on base metals can soon wear away and may cause allergy problems. Manufacturer's catalogues include a good choice of findings, but you will sometimes find it more appropriate to make your own. Always take care to position your findings so that your work is balanced correctly.

1. Jump rings link various jewellery components and findings.

2. Triangle bails are used to hand thicker beads which will not take a jump ring.

3. Eye pins are threaded through beads to link them together and to other findings.

4. Head pins are used in the same way as eye pins.

5. Barrel clasps consist of two halves which screw together.

6. Pierced earwires come in various shapes.

7. Bell caps conceal multistrand thread ends on a necklace or earring.

8. Pin backs provide a base for sewn or glued beads.

9. Posts with butterfly fastenings are for pierced ears.

10. Decorative clasps secure the ends of necklaces and bracelets.

11. Screw and clip fastenings are for unpierced ears.

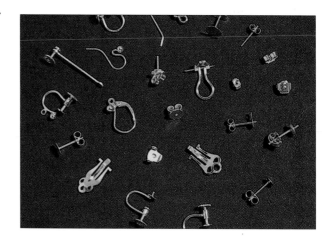

Earrings

You can make earrings in several styles:

• Wire with butterfly fitting

• Wire hooks

• Hoops

• Clips

To make loop earrings for pierced ears, bend up loops of wire using round or half-round pliers. Avoid soldering if possible, but if it is necessary, solder before bending and harden by tapping with the hammer as above.

To make hoops solder a 20-gauge wire to the end of thicker wire, and drill a hole the same size in the other end. Wrap the wire around the top of a mandrel and hit downward until the hoop is springy and the correct size.

Necklaces, Bracelets and Pendants

The clasps you will use are:

• Bolt ring

• Box catch

• Hook and eye

• Spring fitting

• Rivetted joint

Bolt rings are the usual way of fastening manufactured chains. They come in different sizes and work well. After soldering, leave to air-cool, as the spring will become soft if it is quenched immediately.

A hook and eye fastening gives the greatest scope for your own creativity. A simple catch can be made by heating both ends of a length of 18-gauge wire, approximately 4cm (1 1/2 in) long, so that the ends run up into balls. Hold the wire in your insulated tweezers, flux the ends, and concentrate the flame on one end, with a charcoal block behind it. The end will run up into a ball as it begins to melt. Turn it over and repeat the process on the other end. Use round and half-round pliers to bend the wire into a long 'S' shape. Solder up one end with easy solder, and curl the ball on the other end to turn up. Hammer the central area flatter on the anvil to harden it up and improve the appearance.

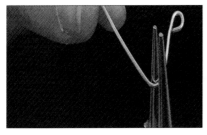

A wire is bent for ear loops.

Bolt ring.

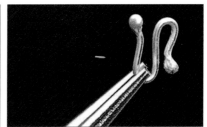

Wire for hook with both ends run up to make small balls.

TECHNIQUES

The great advantage of making jewellery with beads is that you can use fairly simple techniques in different situations and build your work. As we have illustrated in the book, once you have mastered the basic techniques you can use them in lots of different situations and produce very satisfying results.

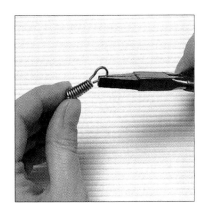
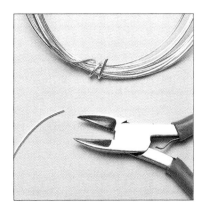

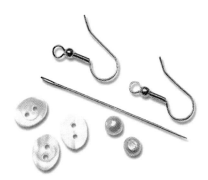

WIRING

1. Making Bead Wires

The first photograph shown right, demonstrates how to hold your pliers so that your control is good.

To make a loop, hold your eyepin or headpin between your finger and thumb, using the other fingers to control it as well. You need about 8 mm ($^3/_8$ in) of wire to make the loop. To make the headpin or eyepin the right length for the loop, either clip off any excess with wirecutters, or "fatigue" the wire by putting your pliers either side of it and gently moving the wire backwards and forwards until the metal breaks cleanly. Put your round-nosed pliers to the top of the wire and roll the wire away from you around the pliers. You do not have to do it in one movement. If you have not made a complete circle, take your pliers out and make the movement again, until you have a neat loop. If you then want to connect this loop into another one, for example to make a double-length earring, open the loop sideways with your pliers, so that you do not damage the metal. The same applies to attaching an earwire; open the loop on the earwire sideways and add the loop on your eyepin or headpin.

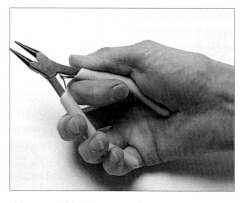

How to hold pliers correctly.

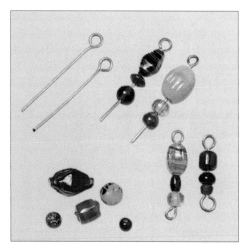

Completed bead wires

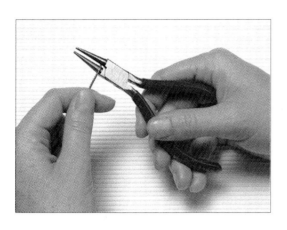

1 Cut a length of wire approximately 2.5 cm (1 in) longer in length than the beads to be threaded.

2 Secure one end of the wire in a pair of round-nosed pliers and carefully bend the wire to create a loop.

3 Thread the beads onto the wire, pushing them up to the looped end of the wire.

4 *Secure one end of the wire in a pair of round-nosed pliers and carefully bend the wire to create a loop.*

2. Wiring a 'Doughnut'

You can, of course, do much more than just roll loops if you are using jewellery wire. It can be incorporated in your designs in many ways. Brass wire is rather springy and is harder to use, but silverplated wire is easier to manage, especially after some practice. Choose 0.8 wire for making decorative coils, or to wire a "donut" and 1.2 wire if you need something more rigid like a hook or a jump ring. It is hard to give precise measurements for wire work, as the items that you are planning to use will all vary. The wire is not expensive, so it is best to cut a piece of wire, keep a record of its length, and then practice and experiment.

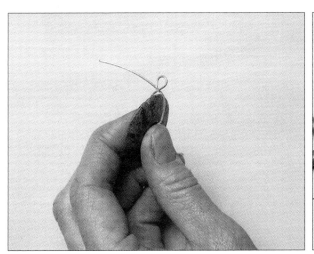

1 To wire a "donut" or something similar, cut your wire similar proportions to those shown in the photograph.

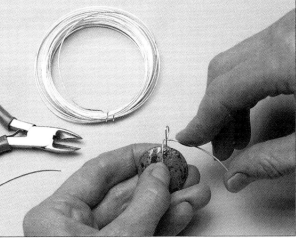

2 Fold the wire through the "donut", leaving one end longer than the other.

3 *Roll the short end to make a loop. Then wrap the longer end around the bottom of the loop.*

4 *Keep wrapping this wire until you have several neat coils, then clip the end, and gently press the top coil in with your pliers to make it neat.*

3. Making a Jump Ring

1 Cut a 15 cm (6 in) length of wire, secure one end in a pair of round-nosed pliers and slowly bend the wire around one side of the pliers to create the beginning of a coil.

2 Continue to coil the wire around the pliers until all the wire is used and a regular coil of wire is formed.

3 Remove the coil from the pliers and, using a pair of wire snips, cut up one side of the coil.

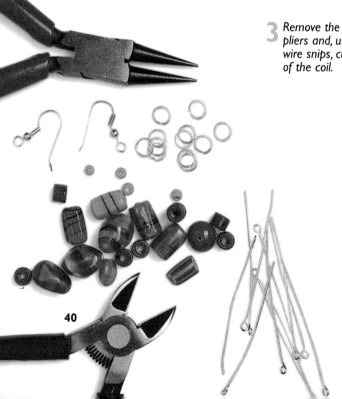

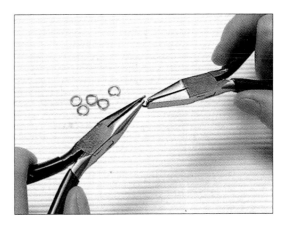

4 *The jump rings can be opened using two pairs of flat-nosed pliers; another jump ring can then be threaded on, and the host jump ring closed.*

5 *A chain can then be created from the jump rings by repeating the process of linking jump rings one after another.*

Jump rings are universally useful in jewellery making.

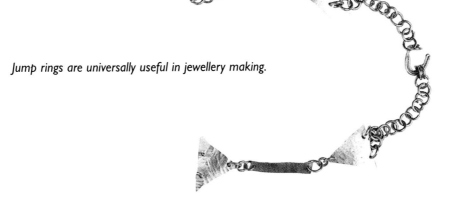

4. Making a Hook

If you are threading beads onto wire and you want a more elaborate and secure loop at the top of them try the following. Bring your wire up, make a loop allowing extra wire, then wrap the extra wire under the loop. Again make several coils and press the end in neatly.

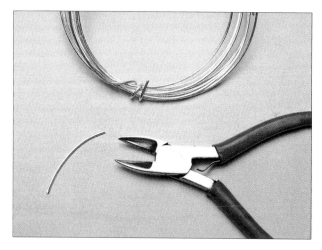

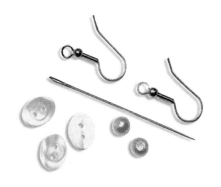

To make a hook, cut a few millimetres of wire.

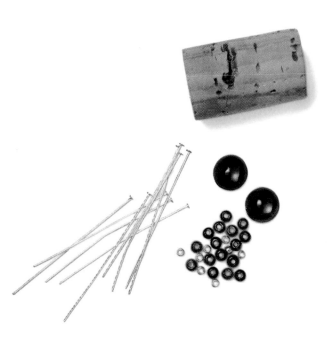

2 *File one end and turn a loop in this end.*

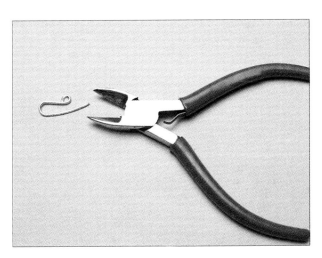

3 Now curve the wire back around your pliers and clip off any excess wire.

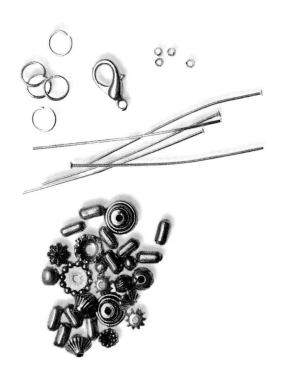

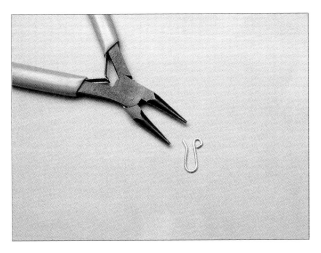

4 Bend up the end of this wire to make a good shape and file this end too.

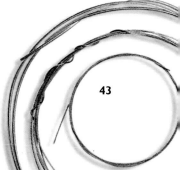

43

5. Twisting Wire

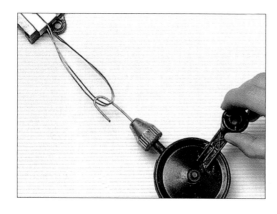

1 With wire snips, cut two equal 120 cm (48 inch) lengths of wire and bend them both in half. Secure the ends in a vice. Take a hooked piece of wire, which is fastened into a drill, and hook it onto the looped end of the bent wires.

2 Turn the hand drill to make the wires twist together. It is important to turn the drill slowly to allow the wires to twist together evenly.

3 Continue to turn the drill until the wires are tightly and evenly twisted together along the length of the wire. You can choose how loosely or tightly twisted you want your wire to be.

4 Remove the twisted wires from the vice and drill. Using the wire snips, cut off the looped end, so that you are left with an even length of wire.

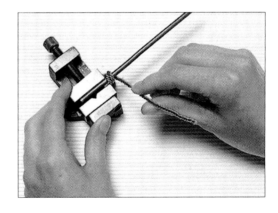

5 Secure a circular rod and one end of the twisted wire in a vice. Slowly bend the twisted wire around the rod.

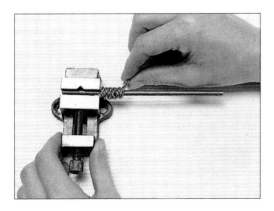

6 Continue to bend the twisted wire around the rod until all of the wire has been used and the wires have formed a coil.

6. Coiling a Loop Fastening

1 Cut a piece of wire approximately 25cm (10 in) in length. Using a pair of round-nosed pliers, coil the wire, starting from the bottom of the pliers and working upwards.

2 Continue to coil the wire along the length of the nose of the pliers, keeping the growing coil tight and even.

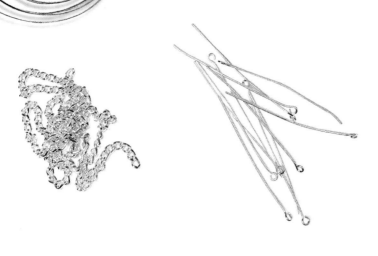

3 Remove the tapering coil from the pliers and use the excess straight wire to form a loop.

4 The loop is created by bending the wire over on itself and tucking the end into the coil. This forms the fastening mechanism.

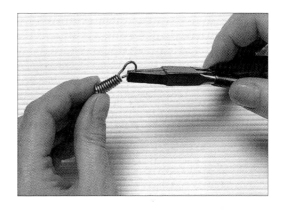

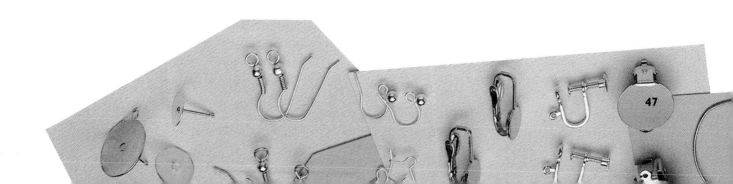

5 *At the opposite and wider end of the coil, use the flat-nosed pliers to bend the very last coil in half at 90 degrees, again making sure that the end of the wire is tucked into the coil. This forms the mechanism by which the fastener is connected to the necklace.*

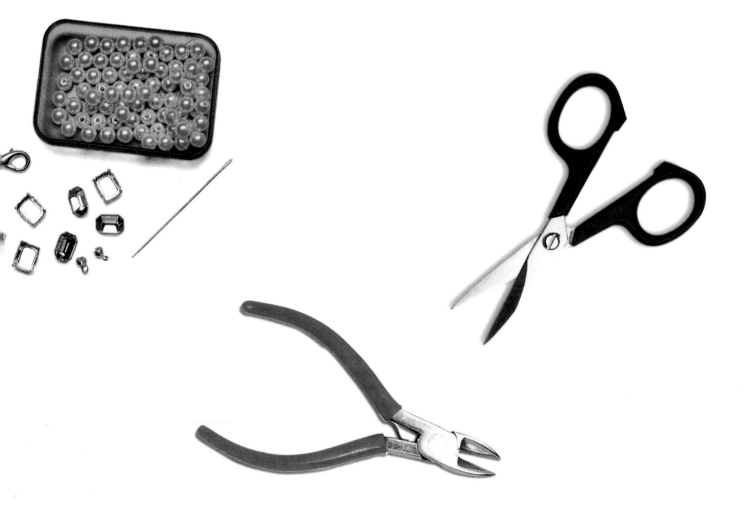

7. Coiling a Hook and Loop Fastening

I   *Cut a length of wire approximately 30cm (12 in) in length. Using a pair of round-nosed pliers, coil the wire, starting from the bottom of the pliers and working upwards.*

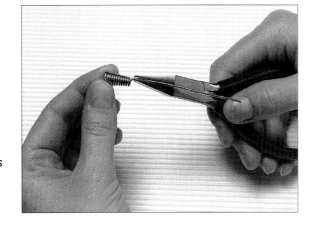

2   *Using the flat-nosed pliers, bend the excess wire at 90 degrees.*

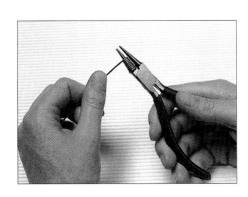

3   *With the round-nosed pliers, bend the wire over, forming a loop.*

4   *Using the tips of the round-nosed pliers, bend the wire back on itself, forming a hook.*

5 Take the flat-nosed pliers and carefully manipulate the bent wire so that it follows the first wire.

6 When the wire is satisfactorily bent, cut off the excess wire with a pair of wire snips and tuck the end discreetly into the coil.

7 At the opposite and wider end of the coil, use the flat-nosed pliers to bend the very last coil in half at 90 degrees, again making sure the end of the wire is tucked into the coil itself. This forms the mechanism by which the fastener is connected to the necklace.

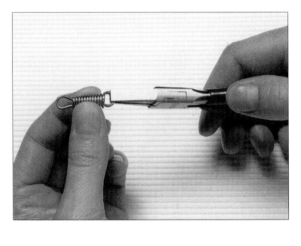

The coiled hook and loop fastening provides a neat finish.

FINISHING

1. Using French Crimps

Leather or cotton thonging can be finished either with knots, or with spring ends or lace end crimps. Spring ends look like coils of wire and you fit them to your thong and press the last coil into the leather with your pliers. The lace end crimps are folded around the thong from either side and squeezed with your pliers.

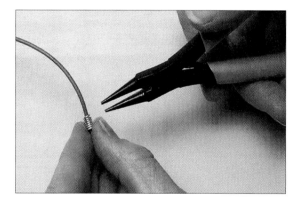

Spring clasps

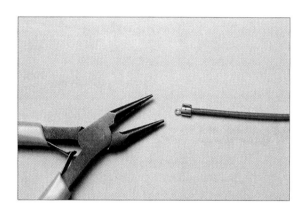

Lace end crimps

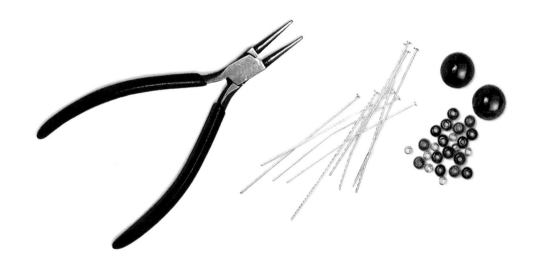

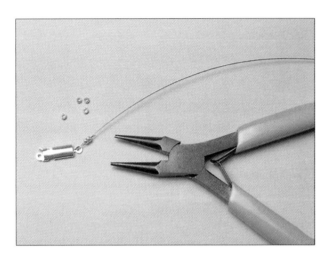

The most simple way to finish a necklace or bracelet is by crimping the ends with French crimps.

1 *Put one or two of the crimps onto the thread that you are using (in this case tiger tail), fold the thread through your fastener, and back through the crimps.*

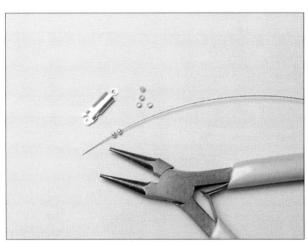

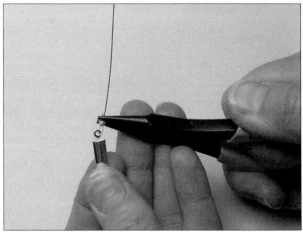

2 *Make sure that your crimps are close to your beads (except on fishing line which shrinks a little) and that your loop is neat but allows movement, and then squeeze the crimps firmly with your pliers.*

3 *Make sure that the crimps will not move on your thread, but do not squeeze so firmly that you damage the thread.*

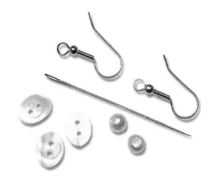

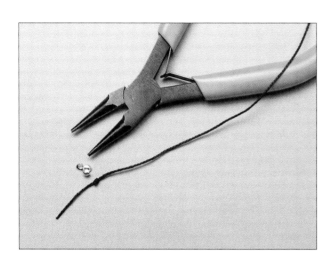

Calottes

Another easy way to finish a necklace is to knot the thread and then squeeze a calotte over the knot and attach your fastener to the calotte. You can put a drop of glue onto the knot before you cover it with the calotte for extra safety, but make sure that the glue does not touch and spoil any precious beads. When you squeeze the calotte again make sure that you do not damage the thread.

53

2. Knotting Between Beads

If you are finishing with a knot and calotte, or using a knot at the end of a tassel, and want to make sure that the knot is close to your beads, put a needle into the knot before you tighten it, then draw the knot back towards the beads with the needle and gently pull the needle out when the knot is sitting next to the beads.

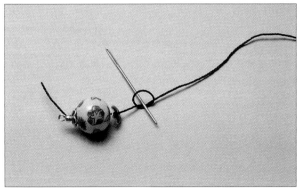

1 To knot between beads, you need to allow approximately twice as much thread as the length of your finished necklace.

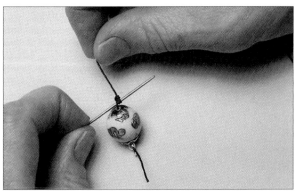

2 The length needed of course, is dependent on the size of your beads and the number of knots, and you should allow even more thread if you are going to have a lot of knots, as it is easier to cut off the excess than to have to reknot due to lack of thread.

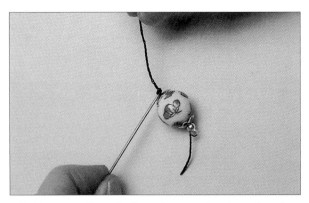

3 Use a needle in the knots between beads so that all your spacing is even.

To make a double knot

If your beads have larger holes you can make double knots to go between them.

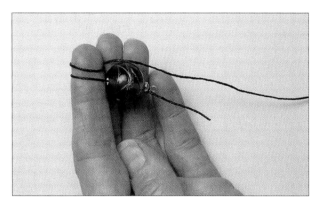

1 *Wrap the thread loosely twice around your finger.*

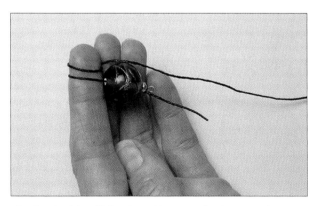

2 *Gently slide off the thread keeping the loops in place.*

3 *Put the needle in the loop in the same way as the single knot and tighten.*

3. Attaching a Fastener

Aswell as being an appropriate way of finishing a necklace, knots are used to attach fasteners.

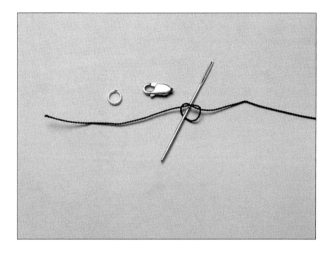

I *To do this make a single knot next to your beads, and leave a needle in it.*

2 *Put on your fastener, leaving space for more knots between it and the knot with the needle in it. Then put the knots into this space, remembering how many you have used, and how much space you left, so that you can duplicate on the other side.*

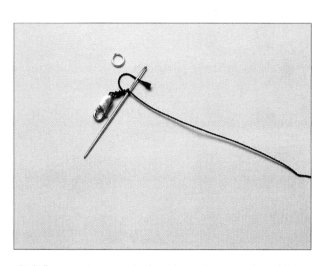

3 *When you have made these knots, put your thread into the needle that you left in the knot, and pull the needle through to tighten everything.*

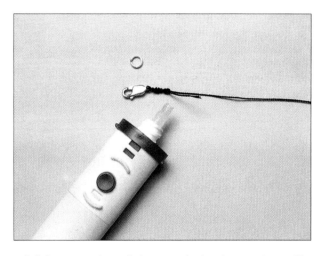

4 *Either put a drop of glue onto the last knot and cut off your loose thread, or if you have large enough holes, thread back into your beads.*

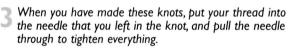

4. Finishing a Multi Strand Necklace

This is a neat and simple way of finishing off a multi strand piece of jewellery.

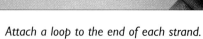

Attach a loop to the end of each strand.

2 *Once all the strands have a loop attached, thread a piece of wire through all the loops, and then thread the end through the loop at the end of the wire as above. Pull tightly.*

3 *To hide the attachment, fit a decorative endpiece over the join.*

4 *Thread a selection of matching beads onto the end piece of wire to finish.*

5. Braiding the Ends

If you have a few special beads, another way to finish them is to braid the ends. The technique that we have used is a simple macrame technique.

1 You need three strands, either single or double. When your strands are ready, leave the middle one in lace and work the left-hand strand under the middle and over the right-hand strand.

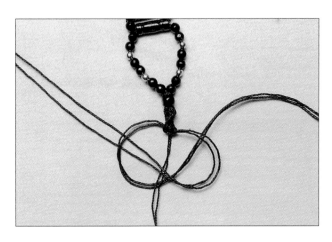

2 Work the right-hand strand over the middle and under the left-hand strand. Continue in this way as the braid builds.

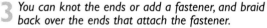

3 *You can knot the ends or add a fastener, and braid back over the ends that attach the fastener.*

Braiding is one good way to finish a multi-strand necklace. Another way to do this is to make loops with crimps at each of the ends, and then pass another thread with a loop at the end through these loops and back into itself. Put a bell cap or a cone over all the ends and either thread more beads onto the single string, or finish on the single string. You can also loop all the single crimped ends onto wire and into a bell cap or cone.

Simple Stringing Project

Before making your necklace you need to decide how long you want it to be – a standard necklace is between 45 cm and 50 cm (18 - 20 in) and a choker 35 cm and 40 cm (14 - 16 in). Next you need to select a suitable thread. There are a number of different types available and the choice depends on the weight of the beads and the size of the hole. Silk, cotton and nylon are all strong and flexible.

YOU WILL NEED

- **Strong cotton thread**
- **2 eye or head pins
  (or silver wire)**
- **Superglue**
- **2 bell caps**
- **Wire cutters**
- **Pliers**
- **Selection of beads**
- **Diamanté roundels**
- **Needle**
- **Necklace clasp**
- **Jump rings**

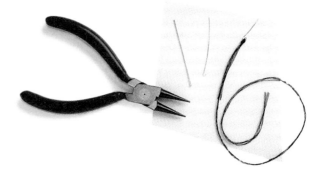

1 *Cut five or six strands of cotton thread to the desired length plus a little extra for knotting the ends. Knot the threads securely through the loop (eye) at one end of an eye pin. If you don't have an eye pin, snip the flat end off a head pin with wire cutters and use pliers to turn it into a loop. Or cut off a short length of silver wire, turn a loop in one end, then knot the threads through the loop as before. Adding a blob of glue to the knot helps to strengthen it.*

2 *To create a neat finish, the pin is inserted through the hole at the top of a bell cap. Trim the pin with wire cutters and then turn another loop using pliers. This second loop is used to attach a necklace clasp (see Step 4).*

3 Having worked out your design, string the beads on to the threads, adding the diamanté roundel spacers to give a little sparkle. Tiny beads or discs can also be used as spacers between beads to create interesting effects. The necklace doesn't necessarily need a central focal bead, but it is essential that the two sides are identical.

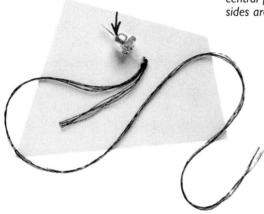

4 This shows in detail how the necklace clasp is attached. Knot the ends of the thread to an eye or head pin as in Step 1, and push through the bell cap as in Step 2. Undo the necklace clasp. Using pliers, open up a jump ring by twisting it sideways. Insert the ring through the loop on one side of the clasp then through a bell cap and then close it up with pliers. Repeat for the second part of the necklace clasp.

6. Linking with eye & head pins

Stringing beads on to thread is not the only way of creating necklaces; they can also be linked together using eye and head pins. This method is frequently used to make earrings, too, and it is very easy to achieve spectacular results. The clever addition of chain links between the beads on this necklace creates a sophisticated finished piece.

YOU WILL NEED

- **Eye or head pins**
- **Wire cutters**
- **Pliers**
- **Selection of beads**
- **Length of chain with wide links**
- **Jump rings**
- **Necklace clasp**

If using head pins, the flat "head" will need to be snipped off with wire cutters, and a loop turned at one end with pliers. Insert a pin through one large bead, trim the wire, and turn a loop at the end. Push a pin through another bead, open the loop slightly and link it to the loop on the previous bead. Continue linking the beads together in this way in groups of two or three.

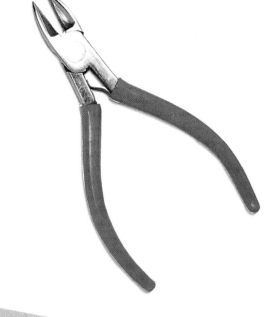

3 Use pliers to open up the loop on one part of the necklace clasp. Push this through the last link in the chain on one side. Close the loop carefully, ensuring the two ends are as close together as possible. Repeat for the other side of the necklace.

2 To attach the chain, first decide how many links are required. Using pliers, open the link one beyond the length required by snipping the join. It is much easier to join a fully closed chain link to an opened loop on the bead than to try and close up an open link. Push the open loop through the chain and close to secure. Continue working in the same way until you have a necklace of the desired length.

65

7. Dividing Strands

A more intricate finishing can be achieved by dividing the strands and working on each individually, before bringing them back together through one bead. The loops created can be as long as you like to suit your design, and you can work on more than two strands if you prefer.

YOU WILL NEED

- **Nylon thread**
- **Pliers**
- **Calotte crimp**
- **Screw necklace**
- **Selection of large and small beads**
- **Diamanté roundels**

Cut two pieces of nylon thread to the desired length plus a little extra to allow for the loops and knotting. Knot the threads together at one end and, using pliers, crimp a calotte over the knot. To do this, separate the two sides of the calotte, slip it over the knot, and shape the ends back together with pliers.

2 *Begin by treating the threads as one and string on beads in the required pattern. Divide the strands then work on each individually, threading beads on to both strands.*

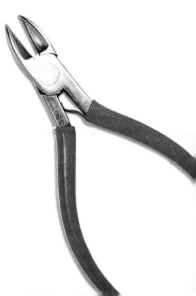

3 When you have completed the loop, bring the strands back together again, threading them both through one bead. Continue dividing and bringing the strands back together again until you reach the length required, remembering to keep both sides of the necklace exactly the same.

4 Knot the ends together close to the beads and crimp a calotte over the knot as before. Open the loops on the screw clasp with pliers and insert them through the loops of each calotte to secure.

67

BEADWORK

1. Freehand Weaving

The other techniques that we have not discussed are the actual beadwork techniques. Beadwork is usually done with rocailles or bugles, or other small beads, and takes the form of either free-hand weaving, such as the Peyote stitch or loomwork.

Free-hand weaving does not have to be done with tiny beads.

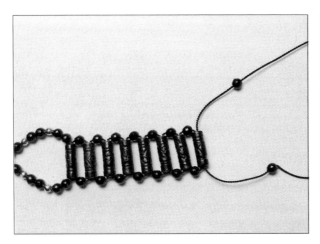

1 To work your beads together as in the example here, use two threads and two needles, and put the threads in from either side of the long beads, so that they cross in the middle.

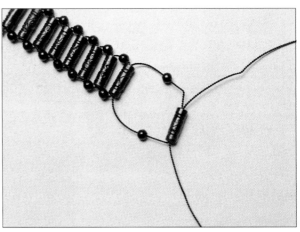

2 Bring the needles back out of the beads, thread a bead or several beads between them, and then thread into the next bead from either side. Keep working in this way.

1a. Fringing

1 You can also make fringing for necklaces, or to go on scarves, by working your threaded needle down through your beads.

2 Add a small bead at the bottom, and then work back up your other beads. They will hang down and the small bead will hold them in place.

Example of a necklace using fringing.

1b. Peyote Stitch

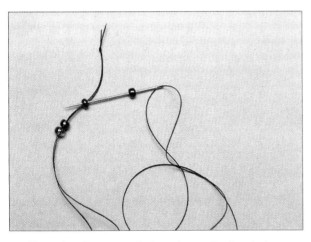

1 To work in Peyote stitch, thread on a few beads (we have used three here)

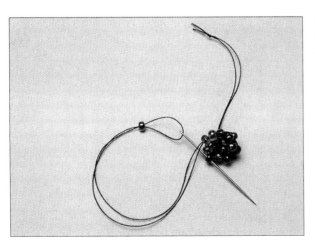

2 Then holding the bottom thread, add another bead and work back into the first bead using the same colour and pull your thread through.

3 Then pick up another bead in the same colour as the second bead and work back into the second bead, and continue in this way, tightening the thread and making a rope of beads.

2. Loomwork

Loomwork is another area that is covered only in its simple forms in this book, though we hope to inspire you to want to learn more.

Loom and materials

An example of a loomwork bracelet

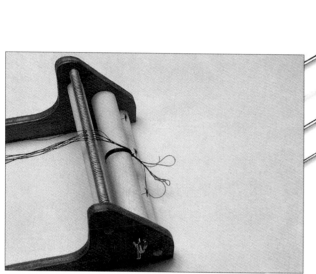

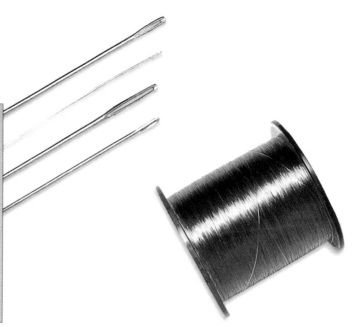

To thread a loom, cut your threads about 25 cm (10 in) longer (at each end) than your work will be and cut one more thread than you will have beads. These are the warp threads. Knot them together and place the knot over the pin on the far end of your loom. Wind them around once or twice so that they are held securely.

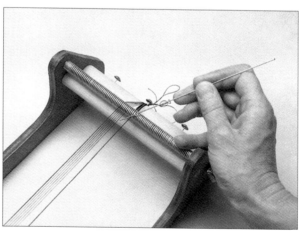

Now bring the threads back towards you, separating them into the grooves on the loom (it is helpful to use a needle to do this). Tie the loose ends onto this end of the loom, so that they are very taut.

73

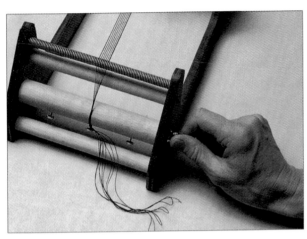

3 If you are making a long piece of work, wind the lengths of warp threads around the roller at the far end, so that it is firmly held, before you tighten your wing nuts, and knot on the loose ends at your end.

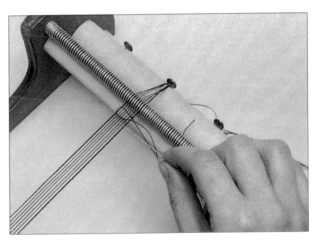

4 To work the beads on the loom, attach your thread to one side, and work a few rows by putting this thread in and out of the warp threads. Then put the beads that you need onto your needle, holding them beneath the warp threads.

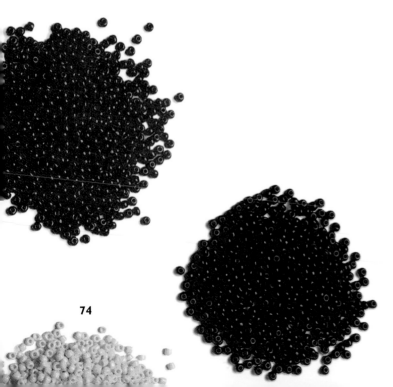

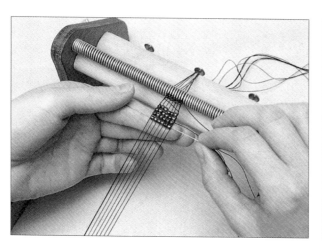

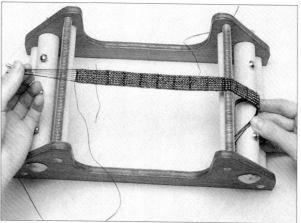

5 Bring the beads up between the threads and pull the thread through, then bring your needle back into the same beads, this time making sure that the beading thread goes above the warp threads. Pull the needle tight at the end of each row so that the beads are held firmly. You will continue to work in this way as you add the pattern to your design. It is sensible to work to the design that you are going to use on graph paper before you start.

6 Before you take your work off the loom, work a few rows with just the thread, as you did at the beginning. Work all your loose ends, and your warp threads back into your strip of beading.

Decorative Effects

Beads are ideal for creating unique decorative effects. Look for smaller beads, which are more suited for embroidery work than for making necklaces. Use them to highlight patterns on decorative braids or to add a glittering finish to ribbon-wrapped combs and bands.

Jewel stones add instant glamour to most pieces of jewellery. Buy them with flat backs, which are easy to glue in position, or cut like genuine precious stones, which must be set in special metal mounts. These stones are made from acrylic or glass and come in a range of sizes, some with holes to allow them to be sewn in place. Both types have mirrored backs and care needs to be taken when handling them as the mirror finish can easily be scratched and spoil the finished effect.

Sequins come in an abundant array of sizes, colours, and shapes and can be sewn or glued directly to any type of hair accessory. Specialist craft and jewellery suppliers include most shapes in their catalogues; some even offer cheap bags of "sweepings" – sequins literally swept from the floor, cleaned and bagged.

Synthetic polymer clay comes in a fantastic range of colours that can be used on their own, or several different colours twisted together to create wonderful marbled effects. Once kneaded to soften and remove air bubbles, they can be rolled out like pastry and cut and shaped with a craft knife. Work intricate patterns into their surface by carefully adding different coloured clays. Paint plain bases with subtle metallic paints to resemble precious metals.

Papier-mâché is one of the most versatile modelling mediums for any form of craft work and jewellery design is no exception. Using the most basic techniques you can cover simple cardboard shapes with newspaper.

Found objects can be used to make fun, innovative hair jewellery and frequently cost nothing at all.

Scraps of fabric and embroidery threads are easy to transform into stylish designs. More unusual materials can be picked up on a visit to a flea market, rummage sale, or antique fair – old watches, broken up, can be used as decorations and to transform something ordinary into a fun, unique design.

Transform unexciting hair accessories into something special by covering them with luxurious ribbons, rich textured braids, or colourful embroidery threads. These can be simply wrapped along the length of a headband or top of a hair comb – colour coordinate one with a special outfit. To hold the ribbon or braid in place securely, place a blob of glue on the wrong side of a headband or comb close to one end, and position the thread or braid over the glue and hold in place while it dries using a small clamp or a clothespin. Finish the same way at the opposite end.

Sewing on sequins.

Bases for Hairslides and Pins

Simple flat-backed bases for hair clips, hair slides and pins are easy to make from polymer and air dry clays, papier-mâché shapes, and fabric scraps. These can then be decorated with paint effects, dazzling bead detail or simple embroidery.

Safety Note

The simplest bases can be shaped from polymer clays. You can use cookie cutters or, with a cardboard template of your own design, cut out the shape carefully using a craft knife. For a three-dimensional effect, layer clay shapes on top of each other. Press them with objects such as a perforated fitting or fallen leaves to create a textured finish. Design a glittering jewel-encrusted finish by pressing glass beads or flat-backed jewel stones into the surface – glass will not melt when the clay is fired. If you are working with several colours, be careful to keep your hands clean to avoid mixing the colours. Use acrylic paints or jewel stones to disguise any faults (water-based colours separate on the polymer base).

Cardboard shapes layered with pasted strips of newspaper, a basic papier-mâché technique, can also become simple bases perfect for painting and decorating with fabric

Marble and pearl pin.

scraps, braids or sequins. Create textured finishes by gluing string or paper pulp in pretty patterns to the base shape, or add jewel stones for a touch of glamour.

Decorate these bases with beads, charms or drops by inserting eye pins or piercing holes at the relevant points. Hang just one beautiful jewel from the centre bottom of the design or dangle several beaded strands. To attach such findings, trim an eye pin

to size (approximately 0.5 cm to 1 cm ($^1/_4$ to $^3/_8$ in), depending on the size of the design) and insert it into the edge of a clay or papier mâché design before it is set. Dab a bit of glue to secure it once it is rigid. Then join wired single beads or groups of beads directly or with a jump ring to the eye pin.

Decorative necklace clasps can also be turned into instant pins by separating the two parts, discarding the plain section, and gluing a pin back to the reverse side. These are often very ornate and can be set with pearls, jewel stones, and diamante. Use the attached loop to hang stunning beads or other charms. You can also adapt large flat, doughnut-style beads typically used as pendants. By looking past the obvious, you can find all sorts of ingenious alternatives.

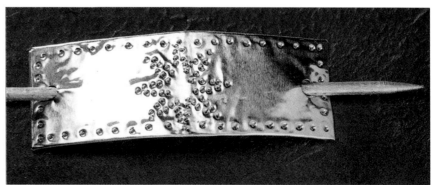

Silver hairclip.

DESIGN SOURCES

The starting point in any design is finding inspiration. Ideas for jewellery designs can come from a visit to a museum or a library. Look to the ancient Egyptian, Roman, and Celtic civilisations, as well as the more recent Arts and Crafts and Art Deco periods, for ideas. A walk in the country or along the seashore can put you in touch with one of the greatest and most economical design source libraries: Mother Nature. Flowers and foliage, rocks and minerals, insect and animal life all can spur the imagination. The sky provides us with the sun, moon, and star motifs that are perfect for interpreting into jewellery forms.

AFRICAN STYLE

African beads come in a variety of materials and designs. Since the earliest days of bone and shell, the continent has developed the famous powder glass and dramatic Bodom beads (Ghana), glass beads (from Bida in Nigeria), clay beads (Morocco), Kiffa beads (Mauritania), dyed bone (Kenya), meerschaum (Tanzania) and beautiful silver beads from Ethiopia.

AFRICAN BEADS ON LEATHER

These are old Venetian glass beads that were sent to West Africa, and old powder glass beads from Ghana. The pendant shows a coin and snakes which are considered to have protective powers.

DECORATIVE CANISTER

This decorative canister takes its inspiration from traditional handicrafts, in which intricately patterned strips are woven to fit snugly over canisters.

KAZURI CERAMICS

Kazuri, which means 'small and beautiful' in Swahili. is the name of a company set up 17 years ago in Nairobi, Kenya, to employ local women to make ceramic beads by hand. They make very dramatic necklaces.

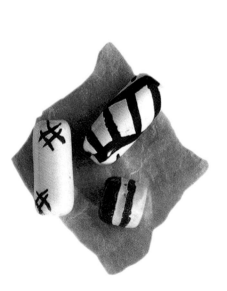

EUROPEAN STYLE

The earliest beads in Europe were made from similar materials to those in other areas, starting with bone, shell and amber, and then progressing into the manufacture of faience and glass beads. Baltic amber has remained very popular. Another early European speciality was the use of jet from Whitby, which started before 1400BC and reached its peak in popularity in Victorian Britain.

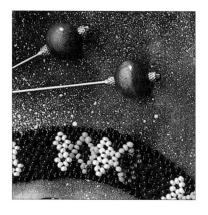

BRONZE AGE NECKLACE

This 7000 year old necklace from Arpachiya, in what is now Iraq, uses cowrie shells. They were originally filled with a red substance which would have contrasted with the shiny black obsidian beads. The top centre black bead is made of mud. The original thread would have been made organic fibre or perhaps animal hair.

GREEK TUBES AND BARS NECKLACE AND EAR-RINGS

The strength of these beads compliment the strong shape of the design.

DECORATED LIGHT FITTING

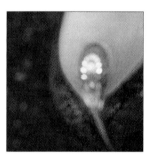

The design of this cheerful bead-fringed lamp was inspired by Victorian antiques.

ART DECO NECKLACE

This long 1930's necklace with tassel pendant and two matching clips, is indeed rife with Arts and Crafts materials and motifs – silver, chrysoprase, moonstone, leafy clusters, coiling wires – but its extreme length, modern style and beaded tassel are very much of the Jazz Age.

SCOTTISH HANDMADE CLAY BEADS

These colourful and intricately patterned polymer clay beads were hand-made in Scotland. They make dramatic jewellery and because the design of the beads is so strong they have been combined here with plain brass washers and a few small brass beads to complement them.

97

FAR EASTERN STYLE

The Chinese are masters in making exquisite cloisonné enamelled beads, as well as beautifully crafted cinnabar beads. Their strong traditions of hand painting and porcelain manufacture have resulted in fine porcelain beads. The Japanese also have a long tradition of bead making, the most well known being the highly decorated Ojime.

The lac and metal beads using Khmer skills, now mainly made in Thailand, are famous. The Philippines produce decorated wooden shell and coral beads, and Indonesia uses natural materials and glass. Bali produces beautiful silver beads.

THAI SILVER EAR-RINGS

These stunning silver beads are made using the traditional skills of Khymer craftsmen, who have come over the borders from Cambodia to Thailand.

AUSTRALIAN 'KOOKABURRA' PENDANT

Australian jewellery in the 19th century used images of local flora and fauna. A celebration of natural surroundings is reflected in this Kookaburra pendant.

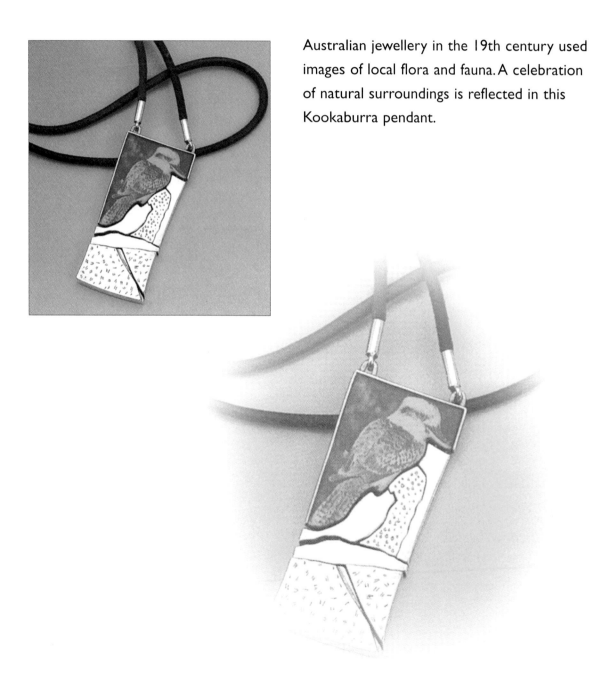

CHINESE NECKLACE

Blue and white porcelain beads patterned with traditional designs are probably the most familiar of Chinese beads.

AMERICAN STYLE

It is the Native American beadwork and work in silver, turquoise and bone, drawing on global inspiration, that is considered most synonymous with North America.

In South America it is the hand painted clay beads from Peru that have become most well-known abroad. There are clay beads and beautiful dyed soapstone beads from Mexico, colourful ceramic beads from Guatemala. Beautiful amber beads come from the Dominican Republic.

In Columbia and Peru, ceramic and stone beads are made using Pre-Columbian designs.

NATIVE AMERICAN BEADWORK

Bead weaving is a quick way of creating intricately patterned jewellery in stunning colour combinations. Bright primary colours work well, as this necklet, bracelet and two simple rings demonstrate.

BRAIDED CORD PENDANT

This simple design achieves its effect with a stunning glass centrepiece and bright modern American glass beads, strung on a cord of braided silks in vibrant colours that highlight the beads.

ART DECO BROOCHES

Some European costume jewellery still bore Victorian or Arts Nouveau motifs (see above). The earrings below have a much more period feel.

MIDDLE EASTERN STYLE

There is an abundance of beads in this area. Egypt is historically important for the faience beads, a forerunner to glass used in ancient Egyptian jewellery and still made there. It is also the earliest known form of beadwork.

Metalworking techniques are skillfully used in these countries to make wonderful beads from silver, gold and base metals, along with lapis lazuli, coral, turquoise and amber.

INDIAN BRAIDED BEADS

This is an effective way to use a few special beads, and makes an interesting change from putting them on leather. Use really bright threads to pick up the colours of the beads and make them look bright and beautiful.

SUMERIAN NECKLET AND ORNAMENTAL DISCS

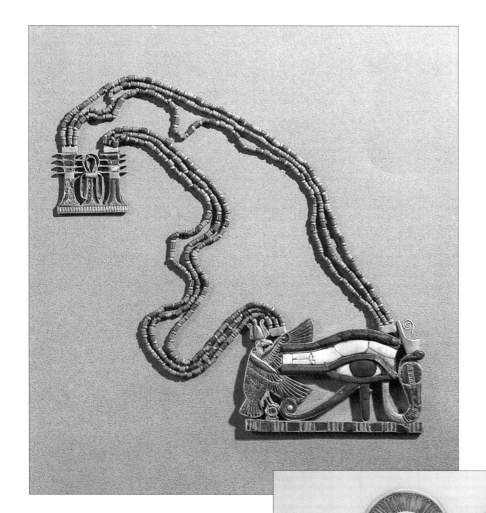

In Egyptian art there
was an overall unity
of proportions
and motifs.

YEMENI-INSPIRED NECKLACE

The inspiration for this piece comes from some wonderful old Yemeni jewellery. White metal beads have been used to make it more affordable and these have been combined with turquoise resin beads and some old Nepalese silver fertility charms to add impact.

WORKING OUT A DESIGN

It is often said that there is nothing new in the world, and it is true that many of the most unusual or innovative pieces of jewellery are inspired by familiar, everyday objects. Inspiration for designs can come from almost anywhere, though frequently inspiration comes simply from the materials to hand.

The past has always been a huge influence on jewellery designers, since not only the techniques but also many of the materials were first used thousands of years ago. The Ancient Egyptian, Roman and Celtic civilisations provide a rich source of inspiration, as do the more recent Arts and Crafts and Art Deco periods. A visit to a museum is the perfect occasion to look at jewellery or be inspired by the renditions of period jewellery in paintings. Libraries are also a good source of illustrated books and old fashion magazines, from home and abroad, with plenty of original ideas to recreate.

Mother Nature produces one of the greatest design source libraries available, and it costs nothing. Flora and fauna, rock and minerals, insect and animal life can all prompt the imagination. The sky has provided us with sun, moon and star motifs, all perfect for interpreting into jewellery, and the sea washes shells up on the beach and sculpts pebbles into interesting shapes. It is a good idea to keep a plastic bag in your pocket, especially when out walking, so that you can bring home anything that inspires you.

Mother Nature produces one of the greatest design source libraries available

Most jewellers use the materials they work with as their source of inspiration. Beads and fabrics can be thrown together haphazardly to create striking and unusual combinations, paints can be experimented with and clays moulded to unusual shapes, depending on the mood of the moment. Turn to ordinary household items – bits of string, spare buttons or scraps of fabric – or simple kitchen equipment such as biscuit cutters or muslin. Many adventurous designers seek inspiration from unorthodox materials.

When you design your own jewellery, each piece will carry your individual stamp, as no two people interpret even the same design source the same way. One of the secrets of success is not to be afraid of experimenting with both the traditional and the unusual, and if you keep an open mind and a sense of humour you will begin to see potential in almost anything around you.

You don't have to draw works of art; rough sketches will suffice

Once you have found your inspiration, try to sketch out different ideas on paper. You will need a sketch book, tracing paper, pencils, coloured crayons, felt tip markers (including gold and silver markers), an eraser and a pencil sharpener. You don't have to draw works of art; rough sketches will suffice. Consider buying a special tray that has channels for the beads to easily plan and make necklaces and bracelets in two or three different lengths.

118

For simple
designs, start with a
centre point of interest,
such as one of the beads
you intend to use. Decide
on the length you want,
then sketch the sides, keeping
them symmetrical.

As a general rule, most necklaces and bracelets should be made from an uneven number of beads so that one will fall at the centre. If you are adding a pendant or tassel decoration, however, use an even number of beads so that the pendant becomes the centre point. To get the best visual balance with beads of different sizes, place the larger ones near the centre and the smaller ones tapering off toward each end. The same principle also applies to any charms.

After working out your basic design, pick the thread, clasp and end fittings. To calculate how many beads you will need, count how many beads fit into 2.5 cm (1 in), then multiply this by the length required. Write down the findings you will need next to your design sketch. If you want to try any unusual paint effects or create complex millefiori beads, experiment with paints on paper before moving on to a sample bead.

FUN & FUNKY
BEAD JEWELLERY

It is so easy to create fashionable, funky, jewellery just like you see in the high street stores. Unusual, fun designs are just as simple to make and will make you stand out from the crowd.

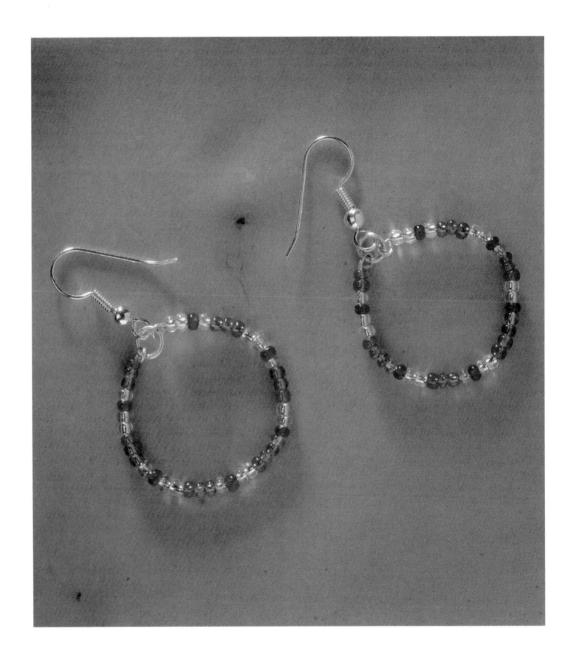

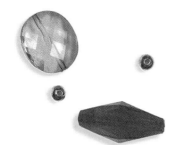

BEADED HOOP EARRINGS

Just a few beads, the most basic findings, and tools are all that's needed to create sensational dangle earrings in minutes. These designs illustrate the basic techniques involved, and once you have mastered them you will find yourself thinking up lots of your own variations. Most of these ideas work best with bought beads but you could mix them with your own papier-mâché or clay designs to add your own personal touch. Look for bead supplier catalogues that not only illustrate the fantastic variety of shapes, sizes, and colours available, but will also provide you with endless inspiration for different bead combinations. Choose beads in colours to match an outfit, an occasion, or simply your mood – crystal, jet and diamante instantly add a touch of glamour for evenings: brighter colours in clashing combinations look fun and funky; pearls mixed with almost anything look elegant and classy.

YOU WILL NEED

- **Jeweller's wire**
- **Wire cutters**
- **Pliers**
- **Glass rocaille beads**
- **2 Jump rings**
- **2 Ear wires**

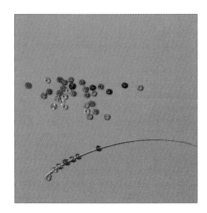

1 Cut a piece of wire approximately 7.5 cm (3 in) long, turn a small loop at one end with pliers, and thread on beads from the other end.

Design Tips

- Take the time to practice turning perfect loops on head pins since this can affect how the drop falls.
- Vary the size and shape of beads to create different visual effects.
- To prevent the head pin slipping through larger beads, use a tiny rocaille as a stopper bead.
- When making your own hoops, wrap the beaded wire around a tube to shape the curve – the tubes that hold small beads are ideal.
- Hoops in different shapes and sizes can be bought from jewellery suppliers and all you need to do is add the beads you want.

2 Leave enough room to turn a loop at the opposite end.

3 Use pliers to open up a jump ring and slip it through both loops to form a circle of beads.

4 Open up the loop at the base of an ear wire with pliers. Slip the jump ring of the bead hoop into the loop and close the loop to secure.

BOLD BEADS & BEASTS NECKLACE

This splendid necklace has been made using an eclectic mix of beads picked up at car boot sales for just a few pence.

YOU WILL NEED

- **A large selection of mixed beads in different sizes**
- **Strong nylon thread**
- **Needle**
- **Jewellery wire**
- **Clasp and calottes from a broken necklace**
- **Pliers**
- **Plasticine**
- **Wallpaper paste**
- **Newspaper**
- **Needle**
- **Crafts knife**
- **PVA glue**
- **Paints**
- **Paint Brushes**
- **Varnish**
- **Eye pins**

127

1 Make a large knot at one end of a thread that is the required length for your necklace. Thread on the beads, mixing them together to create an interesting effect. Crimp a calotte tightly over the knots at each end of the necklace. Attach the necklace clasp using pliers, one section to the loops on each calotte (a bolt ring and split ring have been used here).

2 To make the beaded hoops, cut pieces of jewellery wire to the length required, allowing a little extra for securing the joining to the necklace. Bend one end of each length with pliers, to stop the beads falling straight off, then thread on as required. Bend the other end of the wire then twist the ends together. Join to the necklace by twisting the wire over the thread between two beads.

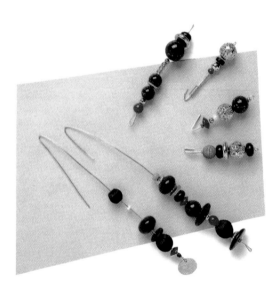

3 Next, cut several different lengths of wire to make bead drops. Loop one end of each piece of wire with pliers, thread on as many beads as required, then use the pliers to form a hook at the opposite end. Attach to the necklace as before.

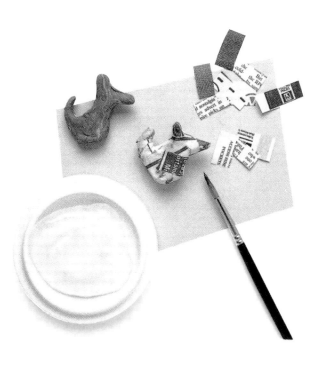

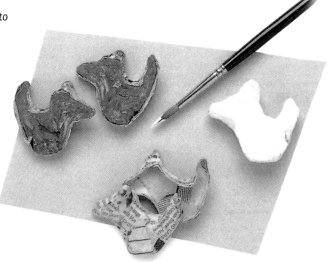

4 *Make a mould in the required shape from plasticine. Make up the wallpaper paste using hot water then tear the newspaper into small, neat pieces. Paste the plasticine mould with several layers of newspaper until completely covered and firm. Leave to dry.*

5 *Carefully cut the papier mâché shape in half with a crafts knife and remove the plasticine. Glue the two halves back together using a PVA adhesive and leave to dry. Make as many animals as you require, then paint each with a white base coat to prevent the newsprint showing through.*

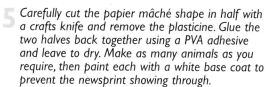

6 Paint each animal, adding features and detail in a contrasting colour, then finish with one or two coats of varnish. When completely dry, carefully pierce the papier mâché animals with a needle from bottom to top. Thread a couple of beads on to an eye pin, then push the pin through the papier mâché and out the other side. Add a few more beads then make a loop at the end of the pin. Thread small beads on to two more eye pins, join all three together to form a long drop, and secure to the necklace by looping the end of the last pin over the nylon thread between two beads.

FISH CHAIN AND EARRINGS

This is a very cheerful piece of jewellery, with lots of blue ceramic fish and fish-patterned beads swimming around your neck. They are even linked with swivels that are actually made as fishing tackle, and then silver-plated for jewellery use.

YOU WILL NEED

For the necklace:
- **10 fish beads**
- **14 fish-shaped beads**
- **24 x 50 mm (2 in) eyepins**
- **28 x 22 mm (1 in) silver plated swivels**
- **2 cm (³/₄ in) 1.2 silver-plated wire**
- **59 x 3 mm silver-plated balls**
- **28 cm (11 in) silver-plated chain**
- **31 x 0/7 grey rocailles**

For the earrings:
- **6 fish-shaped beads**
- **6 x 50 mm (2 in) eyepins**
- **22 x 3 mm (¹/₈ in) silver-plated balls**
- **12 x 0/7 grey rocailles**
- **6 x 12 mm (¹/₂ in) silver-plated swivels**
- **2 x 7 mm (¹/₄ in) jump rings**
- **1 pair earwires**

Tools:
- **Round-nosed pliers**
- **Wirecutters**

1 Make up the straight pieces with your fish beads and fish-shaped beads on the eyepins. Arrange the silver-plated balls and rocailles around the beads.

2 Link the pieces together with the swivels by gently opening the loops on the eyepins sideways.

3 Lay the four lengths of chain and beads together to make sure that the lengths and arrangements are right. Make a large jump ring, as shown in the techniques section, for each end and connect the necklace together,

4 Add a piece of chain to each end, and make a hook for one of the ends. The ear-ring beads are put onto eyepins and then hung from the smaller swivels, and put onto jump rings and the earwires.

DAISY CHAIN BEAD BRACELET

This simple idea for a chain of flowers is easy to work and can be completely transformed by using different-sized beads and colours. Ideally the beads you choose should be smooth, like glass rocailles. This design is one of the easiest to master. If you are looking for more inspiration, look at illustrated books featuring the works of African tribal artisans or Native Americans, or find a sourcebook on Victorian jewellery.

YOU WILL NEED

- **Black glass beads**
- **Silver beads**
- **Strong cotton thread or nylon line**
- **Needle**
- **2 Calotte crimps**
- **Clasp**

To get started cut two lengths of thread to the required finished length for your wrist plus 20 cm (8 in) for knotting and threading. Obtain as many black glass beads and silver beads as you will need to make 6 or 7 flower shapes on the bracelet.

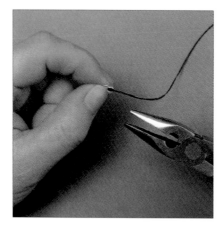

1 Knot the ends of the threads together and secure the knot in the cup of a calotte crimp.

Design Tips

- Experiment by working the same pattern with different sized beads.
- The simple flower shape can also be worked in stunning colour combinations like yellow and electric blue or red and orange. For more traditional flowers, combine white beads with yellow centres or orange beads with black centres.
- Books on more complex bead-weaving patterns are a great source of inspiration for both colour combinations and patterns.
- To make your own bead designs, paint small wooden beads using hobby enamels or artist's acrylic paint.

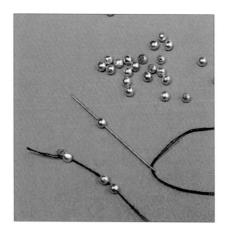

2 Begin the design by threading on 3 silver beads.

3 Next, add 4 black beads.

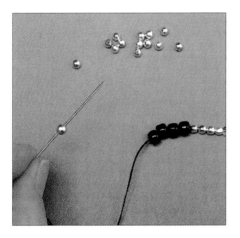

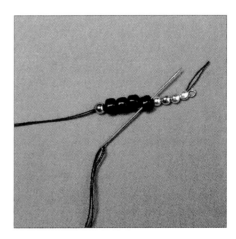

4 Add a silver bead (this will be the centre bead).

5 Take the needle back through the first black bead.

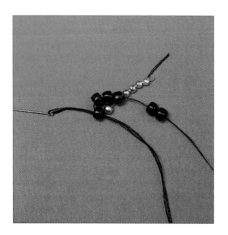

6 Add 2 more black beads and take the needle through the fourth bead. Draw the thread up carefully and push the beads into shape.

8 When you have worked as many flowers as you need, finish with 3 silver beads and knot the thread close to the last bead. Enclose the knot in a calotte crimp, attach a clasp and jump ring to one end, and a single jump ring to the other end to complete the design.

7 Add 3 silver beads before working the next flower.

CINNAMON CLUSTER NECKLACE

A pple coral and cinnabar beads, in three strong strands held by a dramatic centrepiece.

YOU WILL NEED

- **65 brown tile beads**
- **230 x 0/7 black rocailles**
- **80 x 4 mm ($^1/_6$ in) black beads**
- **40 tiny sandalwood beads**
- **19 x 10 mm ($^1/_2$ in) apple coral beads**
- **2 x 14 mm ($^5/_8$ in) apple coral beads**
- **10 nut beads**
- **8 oval cinnabar beads**
- **4 black and red cinnabar beads**
- **1 very ornate cinnabar bead**

1 Cut three lengths of thread about 60 cm (2 ft) long, lay them out and start to plan your design. You will be using nearly all of the beads on the main strands. Keep 3 x 10 mm (¹/₂ in) apple coral beads, 15 x 5 mm (¹/₄ in) black beads, 19 brown tile beads, 3 sandalwood beads and 40 black rocailles to make the centrepiece with the large cinnabar bead, and the ends of the necklace. In this design you will need to keep the centre of the strands quite plain, use smaller beads at the ends of the strands, and space your larger beads evenly through the design. Your strands should be very slightly different lengths, and should hang well together.

2 Finish each end of the strands by making a neat loop with french crimps. Trim off any loose ends of thread. Cut the wire into two pieces and make a generous loop at one end of the pieces. This is opened sideways so that the ends of the necklace strands can be hung from it, and then closed again. Thread a cone onto each of the wires so that the ends of the strands are neatly covered. Add a few more beads to these wires at each side. Then roll the wires and use this loop to attach your fastener.

3 Make the centrepiece by cutting a 30 cm (1 ft) piece of thread and knotting one end. Put a drop of glue onto the knot and allow it to dry. Thread up into the large cinnabar bead, put on more of the smaller beads, and then thread back into the large bead.

4 Finish with the last few beads and make another knot in your thread. Use a needle to draw the knot close to the bottom of the beads, and put a little glue onto this end. Trim the thread close to the knots. You can now loop the centrepiece round the middle of the necklace strands.

WIRE AND MARBLE NECKLACE

Irridescent marbles, wrapped in wire casings, are linked together with loosely coiled sections of wire in this bold necklace.

YOU WILL NEED

- **Wire snips**
- **5.4 m (6 yards) of 1.1 mm (14 gauge) galvanised steel wire**
- **Round-nosed pliers**
- **14 flat-backed glass marbles**
- **Wire**

With wire snips, cut a length of galvanised steel wire 25 cm (10 in) long Using the round-nosed pliers, make a loop in the wire and then carefully wrap the wire around the marble.

2 When the marble is wrapped in wire, make another loop in the end of the wire. These loops connect one section to another. Repeat until all of the marbles have been wrapped.

3 To make the connecting spirals, cut a 13 cm (5 in) length of wire and loosely wrap it around one side of a pair of round-nosed pliers. Bend the top and bottom loops in half.

Link a spiral between every marble section. Join all of the marbles and spirals together securely until they form a necklace.

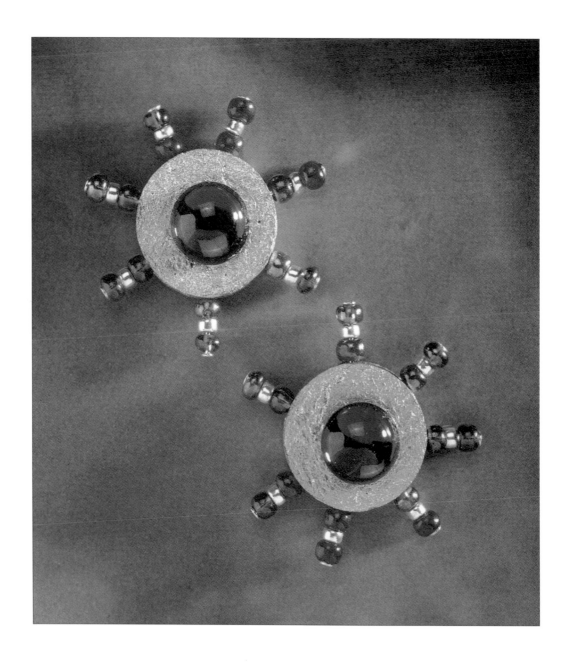

CARNIVAL BEAD EARRINGS

Making something from nothing is a really rewarding hobby and once you get started, you'll find potential in the most unusual objects and delight friends with your creativity. It is surprisingly easy disguising the origins of everyday materials to produce stylish pieces of jewellery. These imaginative earrings are made from slices cut off an ordinary wine bottle cork that are then cleverly transformed with a coat of metallic paint and bead decoration. Cork is a particularly versatile material to work with; you can easily paint it and insert beads on pins into it. The ideas illustrated require no special skills or equipment and can be made in a very short time. Use the designs for inspiration to create your own unique interpretations.

YOU WILL NEED

- **A cork**
- **Sterilising solution or bleach**
- **Cutting mat**
- **Craft knife**
- **Emery board**
- **Gesso**
- **Paintbrush**
- **Gold metallic paint**
- **Darning needle or large tapestry needle**
- **Varnish (optional)**
- **14 head pins**
- **A selection of beads**
- **Wire cutters**
- **Clear-drying hobby adhesive**
- **Epoxy or similar strong adhesive**
- **2 flat-backed jewel stones**
- **2 ear clip findings (or studs if preferred)**

Sterilise the cork before you start the project using household bleach or a sterilising solution from your local pharmacy. Make sure you use clear-drying glue that is suitable for all surfaces.

1 When the sterilised cork is completely dry, cut 2 slices approximately 0.5 cm (¹/₄ in) thick using a heavy-duty craft knife.

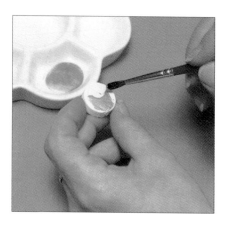

3 Paint all surfaces with a gesso undercoat. Let dry and then add a coat of gold metallic paint.

Design Tips

- Decorate the cork centre with a more intricate painted design and bead the pins with coordinating colours.
- To create a spider-web effect, weave coloured embroidery threads or jewellery wire in and out of the pins.
- For a totally natural look leave the cork unpainted. Just smooth the surface with an emery board and, making sure it is dust-free, add several coats of varnish to bring out the grain.
- Decorate pins with wooden beads to complement the natural look of the cork.
- Once you have mastered the art of making metal spirals, try winding them out from a small bead centre.
- Instead of gluing one striking central bead to the cork, try adding lots of tiny stones at random for a jewel-encrusted finish; then add coordinating bead pins.

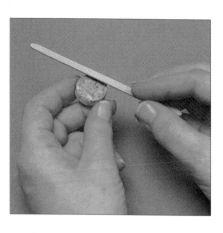

2 Smooth the surface with an emery board. Brush off any dust residue.

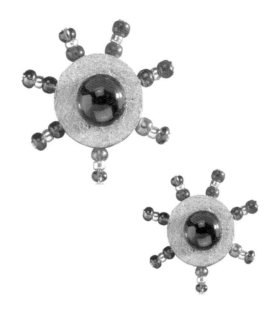

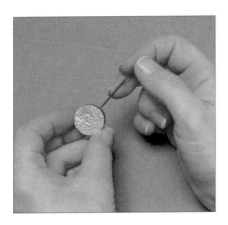

4 Use a thick needle to pierce 7 holes at regular intervals around the edge of the slice. Varnish at this stage if required.

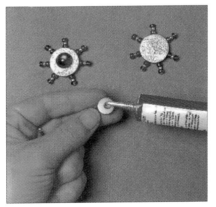

6 Glue central stones and earring backs in place with the stronger adhesive.

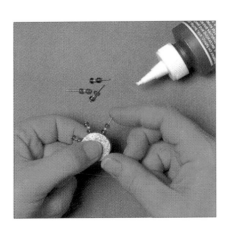

5 Bead each head pin and trim with wire cutters leaving a length of free wire to insert into holes. Add a tiny blob of clear-drying glue to hold the pins in place.

BEAD AND LEATHER BRACELET

Y ou can change the 'earthy' mood shown here by using colourful glass beads or painted ceramic beads from the around the world.

YOU WILL NEED

- **2.3 m (2 ¹/₂ yards) leather thong**
- **Scissors**
- **Hook**
- **Two smaller contrasting ceramic beads**
- **Chunky glass or ceramic beads (quantity depends on size)**
- **Strong adhesive**
- **Wire cutters**

Cut one length of leather thong approximately 46 cm (18 in) long, fold into two and tie a small loop knot as shown. Use the remainder of the leather to thread through the knot before tightly securing.

Place the loop over the hook and start by threading a smaller bead onto the shorter pair of strands. Tie the outer strands onto a bow knot around the bead, once over the top of the inner strands, once below and again above.

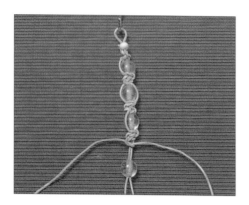

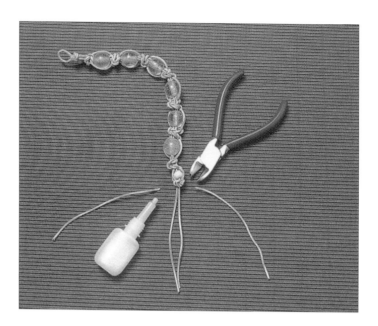

3 Repeat Step 2 but with the larger chunky beads. Stop when the bracelet is about 18 cm (7 in) long.

4 Add the second smaller bead, tie the outer strands and glue into place. Cut remaining outer strands.

TIVOLI EARRINGS

The fabulous variety of beads available in myriad colours is inspiration on its own; it is almost impossible to choose just a small selection. A jar of faceted glass beads in a mix of sizes and a kaleidoscopic range of colours is the inspiration for these ornately beaded earrings. They are much simpler to make than they look and use a clever perforated back that allows you to sew thread in and out. This is then clipped to an earring back to complete the design. The tassels are a dramatic touch but the basic style of these earrings has been around for centuries. When working with such an eclectic mix of colours, it doesn't matter if each earring in the pair is slightly different as long as the overall balance of colour is the same. Points of interest, like the tassels, however, are likely to draw more attention and it is best if these are identical on each.

YOU WILL NEED

- **60 to 70 small faceted beads**
- **6 larger beads for tassel ends**
- **60 to 70 stopper beads**
- **Invisible thread or fine nylon line**
- **Beading needle**
- **2 perforated earring fittings with backs**
- **Glue**
- **Pliers**

Allocated 30 to 35 small, faceted beads and 30 to 35 stopper beads for each earring. The stopper beads, when threaded with the larger beads, secure the larger bead onto the earring fitting. Cut a length of thread approximately 76 cm (30 in) long. (You may prefer to work on shorter lengths and oversew to tie off each end before starting on the next).

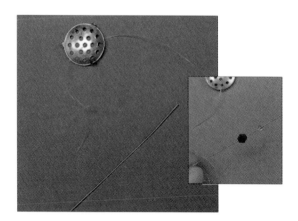

1 Make a large knot in the end of the thread. Take it through the centre hole of the perforated fitting from the concave side and add the first bead and stopper bead.

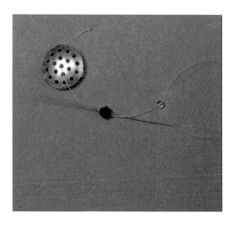

2 Take the needle around the stopper bead and back through the first bead.

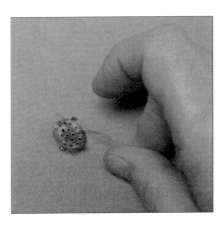

3 Bring the needle back through the centre hole and through the centre of the knot to secure.

Design Tips

- *Divide your selected beads into two groups — one for each earring — to make sure you have a similar mix of sizes and that the overall colour balance is consistent.*
- *You can choose stopper beads to match each bead used or a single neutral colour for all points.*
- *Try varying the length of the tassels or attach beaded loops with a large central bead.*
- *Variations on the theme can be worked with beads of the same colour and varied sizes.*
- *Experiment with different patterns by working in rows from centre point.*

4 Bring the needle back to the right side through a hole adjacent to the centre point. Add a bead and stopper bead as before and take the needle back to the wrong side. Working in circles following the pierced holes on the perforated fitting, continue in the same way until you have completed the outside edge. Depending on the size of your beads, it may not be necessary to bead every hole — you will have to judge this as you go. Oversew the end of the last thread, working the stitches in and out of the holes on the perforated fitting.

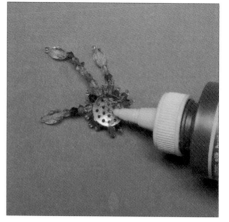

6 Add a dab of glue to all knots and loose ends as a precaution.

5 Position the tassels between 2 claws on the perforated fitting to allow enough room to clamp the claws over the earring back. Make a large knot in a piece of thread 30.5 cm (12 in) long. Thread the needle through the back from the wrong side and add enough beads to make the first tassel. End with a larger bead and stopper bead. Take the thread back through all but the stopper bead and secure on the wrong side. Work the other tassels on both sides in the same way.

7 Clamp the claws of the perforated fitting over the earring back using pliers.

MARBLED BEAD NECKLACE

C reating your own marbled beads is a simple process with today's synthetic modelling clays. There is a dazzling palette of colours available which can produce spectacular results when mixed together.

YOU WILL NEED

- 4 blocks of Fimo or other polymer clay, in contrasting colours
- Crafts knife
- Wooden skewers (satay sticks are perfect)
- Block of plasticine
- Varnish
- Strong thread (coloured raffia is ideal)
- Superglue

1 Break of a small piece of Fimo from one block and knead with your fingers until soft and pliable. Roll it out on a flat surface to form a thin sausage shape, using the palms of your hands. Repeat with the other remaining blocks. Wrap the different colours together to form a plait, then twist the plait and start to knead the colours together.

2 Roll the Fimo into a sausage shape, fold in half, twist the two halves together and knead again. Continue twisting and kneading until all the air bubbles have gone and you achieve a marbled effect.

3 Roll the clay into a sausage shape again. Cut off small pieces with a crafts knife and roll them into balls between the palms of your hands. Make as many balls as you need for the length of necklace required, rolling out more pieces of Fimo if necessary.

4 *Push a wooden skewer through each ball to make a central hole, then gently remove the "head" and insert the skewer from the other end. Smooth any rough edges by gently rolling the head between the palms of your hands again. Thread the beads carefully back on to the skewers and fire in a low oven, following the manufacturer's instructions. Leave to cool.*

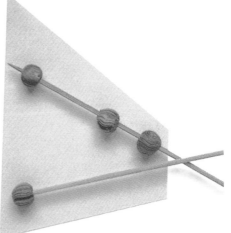

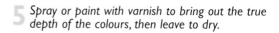

5 *Spray or paint with varnish to bring out the true depth of the colours, then leave to dry.*

6 *Thread the beads on to raffia or other strong thread to the length required. Tie a double knot and fix with a blob of glue. Push the ends back through the beads to conceal them. Alternatively you could intersperse with gold spacer beads and finish with a necklace clasp.*

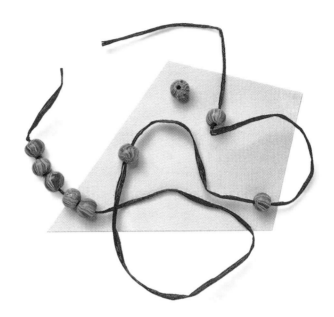

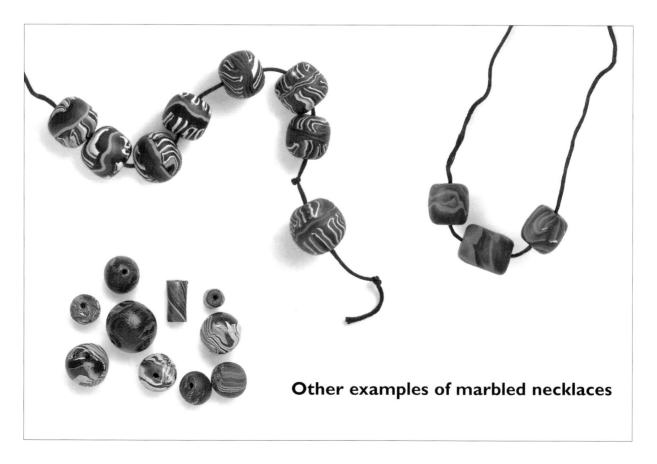

Other examples of marbled necklaces

MULTI-COLOURED CLUSTER NECKLACE

This unusual necklace is made by wiring lots of colourful wooden beads onto a chain with gold eye pins to create a bold, festive design that completely covers the chain. The beads are relatively inexpensive and therefore affordable in the abundant quantities needed to make the necklace striking. You can also use plastic or glass beads, or even make your own out of papier-mâché or Fimo. For a really eclectic mix of beads, collect and string the odd beads you have in your bead box. For more restrained designs, work with a single colour, two-tone colours, or a selection of hues, such as pretty pastels on a silver chain. Mixing together different-sized beads creates yet another look. Once you become skilled at wiring and linking the bead drops to the chain, you'll discover there are endless possibilities.

YOU WILL NEED

- **A length of chain**
- **Multicolour beads**
- **Eye pins**
- **Wire cutters**
- **Round-nosed pliers**
- **4 jump rings**
- **Necklace clasp**

Cut a length of chain to about 61 cm (24 in). To determine how many beads you need, decide whether you join the beads to every link or to every other link, then count up the number of links that you will use. (Ignore the first link at both ends – these will join to a clasp.) Then choose the same number of eye pins.

1 *Thread all but 4 beads onto an eye pin. Add a small stopper bead if the pin slips straight through the hole. Trim the wire to leave approximately 0.5 cm ($^1/_4$ in) for the loop.*

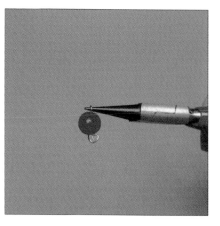

2 *Use the tips of a pair of round-nosed pliers to turn the wire into a neat loop. Thread each of the remaining 4 beads onto an eye pin.*

3 *Trim with wire cutters leaving about 1 cm ($^1/_2$ in). Use pliers to make a loop and then work the wire into a spiral.*

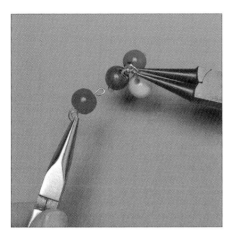

4 Open up a jump ring and thread through the eyes of the pins on the beads with spirals. Close the jump ring securely.

5 Open up a second jump ring and slip it through the first and the centre front link on the chain. Close securely.

Design Tips

- Practice making perfect loops in the top of a head pin using round-nosed pliers. It is important that the loops close securely over the chain links or the beads will fall off when worn.

- If the holes of the bead are too big and the eye pins slip through the holes, add a small rocaille to act as a stopper bead.

- When working with lots of colours or a mix of completely different beads, it is still important to balance the necklace. Too many large beads or beads of the same colour on one side will spoil the effect. Working the necklace from the centre will help you get the balance right.

- Reuse beads from any broken necklaces you have, and look for interesting beads at flea markets, antique markets, or rummage sales.

6 *Open up the loops on the remaining beads and close again over a link in the chain, spacing them as needed.*

7 *Join a jump ring to one end of the chain and a necklace clasp and jump ring to the other.*

PAPIER MÂCHÉ BEADS NECKLACE

The craft of papier mâché is simple to master and can be used to create professional-looking jewellery for very little cost. The beads that make up this stylish necklace were created using the layering technique, then painted in bright colours inspired by Mediterranean china. They can be made in any size and strung into necklaces or wired to make earrings.

YOU WILL NEED

- **Plasticine**
- **Newspaper**
- **Wallpaper paste (with PVA)**
- **Paint brushes**
- **Crafts knife or sharp kitchen knife**
- **PVA glue**
- **Paints in colours of choice**
- **Permanent marker pen**
- **Varnish**
- **Darning needle**
- **Nylon thread**
- **Clasp (optional)**

1 Roll the plasticine into balls, remembering that when finished they will be slightly bigger because of the papier mâché. Roll enough for the length of necklace you want. Tear the newspaper into neat strips, about 4 cm x 1.5 cm (1¹/₂ in x ⁵/₈ in). Make up the wallpaper paste following the manufacturer's instructions but using hot water – this seeps into the paper, making it easier to handle. Brush the paper with paste and wrap a piece around each ball, rolling it in the palm of your hand to seal. Repeat this process about six times until each ball of plasticine is completely covered with paper. Leave to dry.

2 Using a crafts knife or sharp kitchen knife, cut each bead in half. Carefully remove the plasticine from the middle then glue the paper halves back together with strong adhesive. If necessary, wrap another layer of paper over each bead to conceal the join. Leave to dry.

166

3 Decorate the beads in colours and design of your choice. If using a light base colour, cover the beads with a coat of white emulsion or gesso first to prevent newsprint showing through. The design detail has been added to these beads with a black, fine-pointed permanent marker pen. Leave to dry, then finish with a coat of varnish.

4 To make into a necklace, use a darning needle threaded with strong nylon thread, such as fishing line, to string the beads to the desired length. Finish with a clasp or knot securely.

EARRINGS AND A BROOCH

This looks like the work of a master couturier. In fact, the brooch is made from scraps of fabric and thread, sandwiched between hot-water-soluble fabric and PVC, then richly decorated, while the earrings are made from embroidered felt bases.

YOU WILL NEED

- **Scraps of silk fabric and threads**
- **Hot-water-soluble fabric**
- **PVC plastic**
- **Sewing machine**
- **Selection of machine embroidery threads**
- **Scissors**
- **Embroidery hoop**
- **Selection of tiny beads**
- **Gold jeweller's wire**
- **Pliers**
- **Embroiderer's goldwork wire**
- **Superglue**
- **Brooch pin**
- **Small felt square**
- **Selection of larger beads (for drops)**
- **Earwires**

1 Cut out tiny pieces of brightly coloured silk and embroidery threads and put them on top of a piece of hot-water-soluble fabric. Pin a piece of PVC plastic on top of this, creating a sandwich.

2 Drop or cover the feed dog on your sewing machine, according to the handbook, allowing the fabric to move freely. Use a darning foot and thread the machine with a different colour top and bottom. Loosen the spool tension. Machine embroider together in a freehand style, then cut out a circle. This will form the brooch.

3 Place a piece of water-soluble fabric in an embroidery hoop, ensuring that it is held taut, and place the cut-out circle in the centre. Working freehand as before, machine stitch around the edge of the circle to attach it to the water-soluble fabric, then continue to stitch round and round until there is a border of solid stitching around the circle about 6 mm ($^1/_4$ in) wide. Sew in the ends of the thread to neaten. Cut out the shape then put it in a shallow dish and pour boiling water over it until it shrinks. Leave to cool in cold water, then squeeze out excess water in a towel and leave to dry.

4 Thread strings of tiny beads in varying lengths and use to decorate the outer edge of the brooch. Take the thread back through all but the very last bead in each string and stitch in place so that the strings radiate out. Make a coil of gold wire with pliers and stitch it to the centre, then stitch small pieces of goldwork wire around the edge with beads scattered in between. Glue or stitch the brooch pin in position.

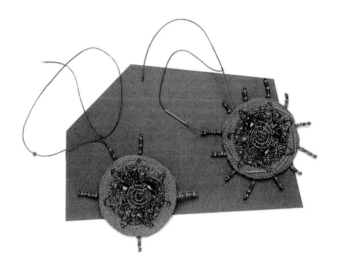

5 Cut three heart shapes from felt, making them slightly larger than the required size. Tightly fix a piece of water-soluble fabric in an embroidery hoop and, with the sewing machine set for freehand embroidery as before, stitch each heart to the fabric around the edges.

6 Stitch up and down each heart from side to side until the felt is completely covered. Stitch around the edges again to strengthen. Cut out the shapes and simmer them in a saucepan of water for about 5 minutes. Cool in cold water, squeeze out the excess water in a towel and leave to dry.

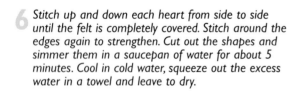

7 To make the drop for the brooch, cut a piece of wire to the required length. Thread on some beads and use pliers to bend both ends of the wire to form a hook. Make a hole in the top of one heart and push a hooked end of wire through. Use pliers to close the hook and secure the heart. Make a hold in the bottom of the brooch and secure the other end of the wire in the same way.

8 Use pliers to make a decorative wire coil for the bottom of each earring, threading a bead on to the top of each and then bending to form a hook. Cut two smaller pieces of wire, thread on some beads, and use pliers to make hooks at each end. Make a hole in the top and bottom of the two remaining hearts and fix the coils to the bottom and the beaded wire to the top, closing the hooks as before. To finish, attach ear wires and close the hooks to secure.

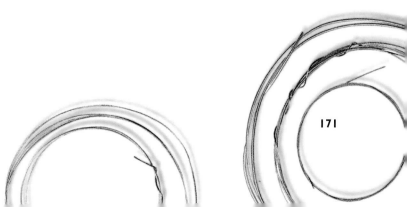

HANDPAINTED PAPER NECKLACE

Y ou might remember tearing strips from
magazines or catalogues to make paper bead
necklaces when you were a child. Now you can make
more sophisticated paper beads that even resemble
pretty ceramic beads by choosing the right paper and
using the right techniques. The skills to make these
beads are easy to master, and once you've had a little
practice you can have a wonderful time creating lots
of different effects. Experiment with unusual papers as
well as with traditional wrapping papers. Shiny foil
designs, textured handmade papers, and even your own
hand-painted plain paper can all be used to great effect.
You can vary the shape of each bead by cutting paper
strips to different lengths, widths, and shapes – the
longer the strip, the fatter the bead, and the wider the
strip, the longer the bead.

YOU WILL NEED

- **2 large sheets of paper**
- **Poster paints in several colours**
- **Large paintbrush**
- **Pencil**
- **Long ruler**
- **Scissors**
- **Toothpick or wooden skewer**
- **PVA glue**
- **Spray or paint-on varnish**
- **Needle**
- **Nylon thread**
- **2 calotte crimps**
- **Gold spacer beads**
- **1 head pin**
- **3 jump rings**
- **Necklace clasp**
- **Pliers**

These beads are made from painted paper cut into 2 different shapes, and then rolled and glued. Use 2 sheets of paper, about 41 x 46 cm (16 x 18 in) in size. Cut nylon thread for the necklace into a length of 61 cm (24 in), with a little extra for knotting.

Lay the sheet of paper out on flat surface and paint on a stripe design. Leave to dry. Paint another sheet of paper in one of the colours used in the stripe design and use the tip of the brush to add texture. Leave to dry.

Lay the striped paper face down with the stripes falling vertically. Mark one edge of the paper in 2.5 cm (1 in) intervals. One the opposite edge, mark 1 cm ($^1/_2$ in), then mark 2.5 cm (1 in) intervals. Connect the marks on opposite edges of the paper, forming long triangles. Lay the plain painted paper wrong side down on a flat surface and mark on the vertical edge intervals of 1 cm ($^1/_2$ in). Use a ruler to join the marks together in parallel lines.

Design Tips

- *Spray or paint beads with couple of coats of varnish to give them a more durable finish.*

- *For totally unique beads, paint large sheets of paper with your own designs, experimenting with different paint effects, such as marbling, sponging, striping, and stippling.*

- *To add a decorative touch, run a metallic pen along the edge of each paper strip before rolling up.*

- *If you make your own paper, add interesting texture to the paper with ends of coloured thread, fabric bits, herbs, flowers, and grasses.*

- *Recycle wrapping paper and colourful magazine pages for beads that cost next to nothing – if you don't like the finished effect, you can always paint them with acrylic paints or even nail polish.*

3 Cut out the strips you need. Discard outside edge strips. Roll triangles around a toothpick, starting at the widest end. Keep the roll tight with the tapering edges in the centre. Roll the straight strips around a toothpick to form cylinder-shaped beads.

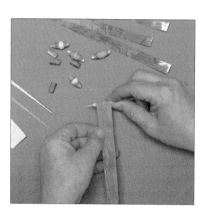

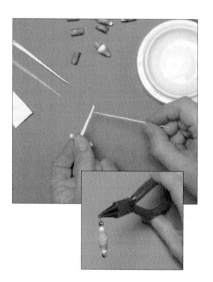

4 Before the end of the bead, dab a little glue on the wrong side, then continue rolling. Hold until secure and slide off the toothpick. To make the beads last longer and look glossy, spray or paint with varnish. Make a central pendant by threading a gold bead onto a head pin, followed by a paper bead and another gold bead. Turn a loop in the top of the pin using round-nosed pliers, trimming any excess wire.

5 Make a large knot in one end of the thread and place inside a calotte crimp. Close the calotte using pliers. String the paper beads onto the thread, alternating with gold spacer beads. Add the pendant when you reach the centre front point, and work the second side of the necklace to match the first. Add a clasp and jump ring to the loops on the calotte crimps at the ends.

FUN & FUNKY
BEAD DECORATION

Add an individual touch to everyday items around the house – this will really brighten things up.

You could even add your own touch to a plain item of clothing or accessory which would make great gifts that no-one else could buy!

DECORATED BOX

S imple decorations make a plain box look opulent and exciting.

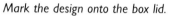
Mark the design onto the box lid.

2 Use paper glue to stick the beads onto the box. Start with the ridges sides. Put glue into some of the grooves and then put two bugles and a gold rocaille into each one.

3 Stick on the central glass cabochon. Then start gluing beads along the straight lines on your box lid. Use your needle to position the bugles with a gold rocaille between each one.

4 Spread more glue into the centre of each triangular section. Position a few more bugles in these sections. Sprinkle the gold rocailles liberally onto the rest of the glue. Now work on the other sections of the box. When you have finished the design, check the positioning of all the beads and leave the box to dry.

HARLEQUIN MASK

Variation on a Theme – Gluing

YOU WILL NEED

- 1 packet green sequins
- 1 packet turquoise sequins
- 1 packet blue sequins
- 1 packet purple sequins
- 1 packet pink sequins
- 1 packet light pink sequins
- 1 packet silver bugle beads
- 1 packet gold bugle beads
- 1 packet red bugle beads
- 1 packet blue bugle beads
- 1 packet transparent rocaille beads
- 1 packet gold rocaille beads
- 1 packet metallic purple rocaille beads
- 1 packet small gold beads
- 8 flat, mirrored beads (we used four triangles, two squares and two ovals)
- Beading thread
- Beading needle
- Dressmaker's chalk pencil
- 1 mask
- Clear, all-purpose glue
- 1 silver glitter glue pen
- 1 gold glitter glue pen

Masks used to be worn at balls so that strangers could flirt, untrammeled by conventions. Use an imaginative mix of beads and sequins to revive an old custom and transform a mask.

To decorate the mask, use the dressmakers chalk to draw a diamond grid onto the mask, leaving 5 mm (¹/₄ in) border all around the edge and around the eye holes. Work on one diamond-shape at a time and apply a thin layer of glue to the mask, then carefully apply sequins using a needle. Overlap them slightly until you have covered the whole diamond.

When you apply the bugle beads, use a beading needle to guide them into position. Add one bead at a time and finish one row at a time. It is worth threading sufficient rocailles on a needle to cover one edge of a diamond shape. Continue until you have covered the whole diamond.

You can achieve a variety of effects by gluing down the beads in different directions within individual diamonds. Fill in some of the diamonds with glitter glue pens, using as many techniques and colours as you wish to create an interesting, multi-coloured surface.

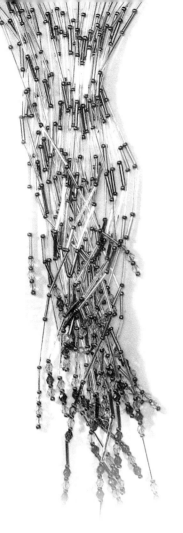

BEAD CURTAIN

You can use beads to great effect as window decoration. It is sensible to choose reasonably inexpensive beads as even a small curtain will require a lot of beads. The effect is very rewarding. We give dimensions and numbers of beads for the curtain illustrated, but if you want a different-sized curtain you will obviously need to adjust these.

YOU WILL NEED

- 1 ft 4 in (40 cm) angled doweling
- 29 x 4 ft 6 in (135 cm) polyester thread
- 284 silver bugles
- 79 dark blue bugles
- 145 turquoise bugles
- 81 green bugles
- 28 x 5 mm ($^1/_4$ in) faceted beads—light blue
- 32 x 5 mm ($^1/_4$ in) faceted beads—green
- 34 x 5 mm ($^1/_4$ in) faceted beads—dark blue
- 14 x 6 mm ($^1/_4$ in) faceted beads—light blue
- 600 x 0/7 rocailles
- 60 french crimps
- Wood stain or permanent marker
- Fine needle
- Scissors
- Necklace pliers
- Bradawl

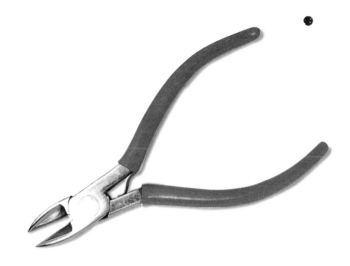

1 Cut the piece of wood to length and make sure that it does not have rough ends. Then stain it. We used a permanent marker, so you could stain to a colour to match the beads, or your room.

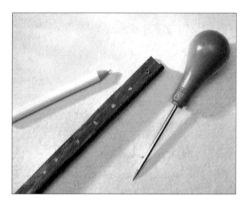

2 Work out how many strings of beads you are going to hang and measure along the top of your wood. Then make holes through the wood with a bradawl.

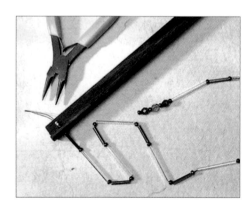

3 Thread one rocaille into the middle of your pieces of thread, to hold the beads at the bottom, then thread double through the other beads.

4 Bring the threads up through the wood and put two crimps onto the top of the threads to hold them in place. The crimps will be hidden by the angled wood. Hang the curtain from right-angled hooks.

LAMP SHADE
Variation on a Theme – Threading

Lampshades are one of the easiest home accessories to customise with beads, enabling you to put your own creative stamp on an interior.

The rich looking bead fringe on the left was worked in a simple pattern using colours to coordinate with the shade. Two differently patterned strings were alternated all round, each being threaded to cotton, which hangs more freely than nylon and worked from the bottom upwards.

YOU WILL NEED

For both shades:
- **Braid or tape**
- **Cotton**
- **Bradawl**
- **Crystal beads**
- **Wooden disc beads**
- **Double sided adhesive tape**
- **Nylon thread**
- **Needle**
- **Glue**

Cut a piece of braid or tape to fit the shade, allowing for securing and turning in raw edges. For each string, cut a length of cotton a little more than twice the required length. Thread one end through the base bead, then both ends through the rest of the beads. Overstitch the thread to the wrong side of the braid, so that the top bead site just below the braid. To finish, wrap the braid around the bottom of the shade and stitch it securely in place. Alternatively, use double-sided adhesive tape to secure the braid to the shade.

To make the trim for the parchment shade below, string the beads on to nylon thread – the finished length will need to be the circumference of the bottom edge of the shade plus at least half as much again, depending on the width and depth of the drop. To secure the string, first pierce holes at regular intervals around the bottom of the shade, through the binding, to prevent the shade from tearing. Next, fold the nylon thread double at the point the drop is to start and push this loop through the hole to the wrong side. Overstitch the loop firmly to the binding, adding a small blob of glue to secure. Once the string is in place, glue wooden disc beads over the holes to give a neat finish.

WIND CHIMES

Variation on a Theme
– Threading

Simple bone beads, carved with exotic patterns, along with cinnabar and silver beads, make beautiful wind chimes. Hang them by your door or window and enjoy their soft sounds as they sway in the breeze.

YOU WILL NEED

- **Plastic curtain ring**
- **String/raffia twine/cord**
- **Assorted beads**
  (cinnabar, silver and bone)
- **Invisible nylon line**
- **Scissors**

The mix of subtle, neutral colours highlighted with cinnabar and silver emphasises the design of these simple chimes. They were hung from a cheap plastic curtain ring bound with fine string to enhance the natural theme. You could steep the string in cold tea for a few hours to darken it subtly, or use raffia, twine or brightly coloured cord to bind the ring if preferred.

For the outer ring, make up six bead strings on strong, invisible nylon line, each measuring approximately 25 cm (10 in) when completed. To do this, cut the six threads into lengths of 60 cm (24 in), fold each in half and take one end of the thread through the rest of the beads.

Tie and knot each of these securely to the plastic ring. Bind string tightly round the ring to cover it completely, taking the string across the centre and back again to form the middle bar.

To make up the centrepiece, start with three strings. Bring these together at the top by threading all the ends together through more beads. Plait three lengths of string together to make the hanging tread, and knot this and the centrepiece to the middle bar. The finished windchimes will add a restful touch to any corner of your home.

CURTAIN TIE-BACKS

These tie-backs have been made much more individual and interesting by adding beads. These should only be considered inspirational, as you will find different tie-backs and your colour schemes will vary.

YOU WILL NEED

- **Polyester thread**
- **Assortment of beads**
- **Strong needles**
- **Scissors**

1 For the top of this tie-back use rocailles to 'anchor' the big rust beads, making them rather like exotic fruits.

2 Beneath the rust beads are natural wooden beads, with a rocaille on either side of them. Think here of your positioning so that the beads are evenly spaced.

3 *The final section has black glass beads sewn into the little loops on the tie-backs.*

For a more luxurious feel, why not try using a gold braid as a base on which to decorate.

HAT BAND

I f you do not want to have beads all over your hat, another good idea is to make a hat band with beads. We have used glass beads with a lovely sheen to them, with a Peyote stitch to weave them together. This does require patience, but the band looks stunning.

YOU WILL NEED

- About $^3/_4$ oz (20 g) each of three colors of 3 mm ($^1/_8$ in) beads
- 1 x 10 mm ($^2/_5$ in) bead for the rosette
- polyester thread
- Fine needle
- Scissors
- Glue

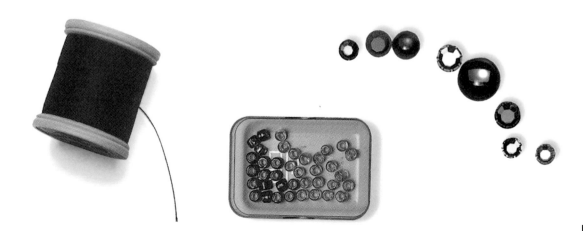

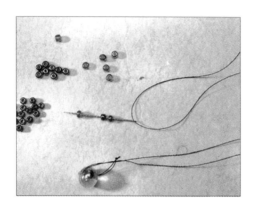

1 Cut a 150 cm (5 ft) length of thread, knot the end and work it double through the large bead. Thread on one each of red, green and blue beads in sequence, repeat four times, and pick up the knotted end of the thread to hold the beads in place.

2 Work on from here, threading red into red etc. for five rows, making a rosette round the large bead. Leave the end of the thread in place.

3 Thread red, green and blue beads onto a new long thread and then thread back into them with the same colour so that you make a spiral of beads. Keep working in this way until you have created the right length for your hat, with the rosette between the two ends. The spiral of beads will be quite stretchy, so make sure it does not get too long. When you knot on a new thread it is a good idea to put a drop of glue onto the knots as the polyester is very slippery. Always try to avoid getting glue onto the beads.

4 Use the thread at the end of the spiral to weave through the rosette to join them, then use the loose thread from the rosette to work into the beginning of the spiral to join the circle completely.

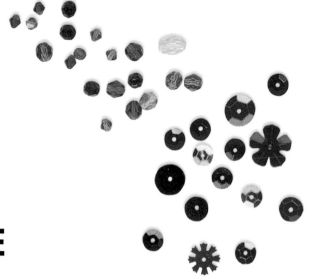

BEADED HAIR SLIDE

This beaded hair slide has a dazzling effect from a distance.

YOU WILL NEED

- **Tiger tail**
- **Faceted blue beads**
- **Calotte crimp**
- **Barrette base**
- **Needle-nosed pliers**

Look for a base that suits the thickness of your hair and that holds your hair in place for your chosen style. Measure the length of the base to gauge how many jewels you will need.

Cut three lengths of tiger tail. Slip one end of each through the hole at one end of the clip and secure with a calotte crimp – this gives a neater finish than knots.

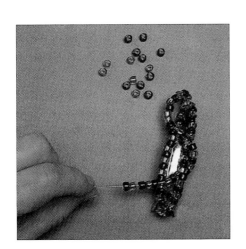

Thread beads on each of the outside threads and attach to the opposite end of the barrette with a calotte crimp as in Step 1. Bead the middle thread and work it over and under the others to create a woven effect.

Just a few special beads mimicking classic china designs look sensational when glued in place. Create designs using the same type of beads, or mix coordinating colours and vary the way they are placed to achieve more original effects.

5.7
CLASSIC CHIC
BEAD JEWELLERY

Jet, pearl and amber are just some of the stunning materials used to make the designs in this chapter. Eye catching black and white designs look forever stylish, whilst the more colourful designs still have a classic feel.

CABOCHON EARRINGS

These elegant earrings are a perfect example of how easy it is to make your own jewellery. The beads are simply threaded on to a head pin and then joined to an ear clip with a jump ring. Special flat-backed beads known as cabochons are a stylish way of concealing the ear clips.

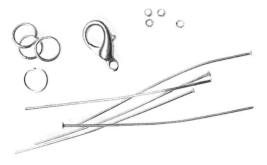

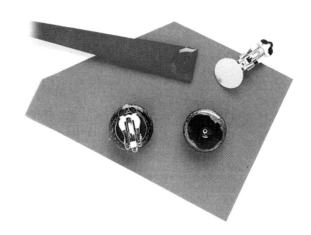

1 Glue an ear clip to the back of each cabochon so that the loop protrudes just below the bead. Leave until completely dry.

2 Thread a small rocaille on to each head pin to act as a stopper and prevent the pin slipping straight through. Add a large bead, a few more rocailles, another large bead and, finally, another rocaille. Trim the wire with wire cutters if necessary and turn a loop with the pliers.

3 Open a jump ring with the pliers and insert it through both the loop at the top of the head pin and the loop on the ear clip. Close carefully, making sure the two ends meet.

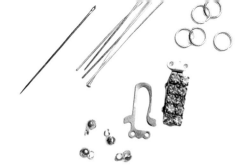

'JET' AND DIAMANTÉ BEAD CHOKER

The classic combination of jet and diamante has existed in jewellery design for centuries. Real jet beads are expensive, but you can recreate the look with imitation replicas in glass or plastic. Faceted glass beads are the best choice; they are heavier and have a more realistic finish than their plastic equivalents. You can make a simple but striking necklace by just stringing the beads together with diamanté rondelles placed between each bead or bead group. More intricate designs, like the jet and diamante necklace described here, have a greater impact especially when worked on several strands threaded through dramatic diamanté spacers. This design is also finished with an old clasp to give it the look of a genuine antique. Start a collection of unusual clasps to add a special finish to any of your designs.

YOU WILL NEED

- **Strong black cotton thread**
- **4 Calotte crimps**
- **Round-nosed pliers**
- **Needle-nosed pliers**
- **Sewing needle**
- **Small black, faceted beads and diamanté rondelles**
- **5 x 3-hole diamanté spacer bars**
- **5 x head pins**
- **5 x jump rings**
- **Necklace clasp with 2 holes**

To make this 36 cm (14 in) choker, cut black cotton thread into 4 strands of 51 cm (20 in) each. Use the extra 15 cm (6 in) for knotting and easy threading. The diamanté spacer bars have 3 holes: 2 holes for threading strands of double thread, and a third hole to join a jump ring and hanging beaded pin.

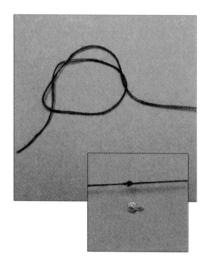

1 *Knot the threads together in pairs. Secure each knot within a calotte crimp.*

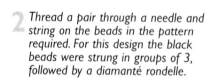

2 *Thread a pair through a needle and string on the beads in the pattern required. For this design the black beads were strung in groups of 3, followed by a diamanté rondelle.*

3 *Work the bead pattern to the start of the centre design and replace the rondelle with a spacer bar, taking the needle through the top hole.*

Design Tips

- To avoid any pitfalls, work out more complex designs on paper before starting this necklace.
- Measure your neck with a longer bead necklace or a string, following the curve of your neck.
- Avoid making the necklace too short or it will look like it is strangling you.
- Diamanté rondelles and spacers are quite expensive, so use them sparingly between groups of beads or substitute with tiny faceted crystal for a similar effect.
- Scour antique markets, flea markets, and rummage sales for old clasps or necklaces that you can restring.

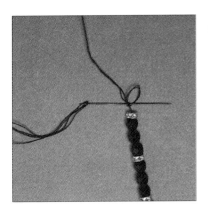

4 Add two beads and take the needle through the next spacer bar making sure it goes through the top hole again. Repeat until all the spacer bars are threaded on. Complete the string to match the first side. Use a needle to pull the knot close to the last bead.

5 Work the second thread pair in the same way.

6 Thread alternating beads and diamante rondelles onto a head pin and turn a loop at the top of the pin with round-nosed pliers. Open up a jump ring and push it through both the bottom loop of a spacer bar and the loop on the beaded pin. Close to secure and attach the loop on each calotte to the holes on the necklace clasp, opening and closing them with pliers.

PIERCED BEADED BROOCH

The sieve or pierced brooch finding used here comes in two parts: a pierced front section with claws, which can be embroidered with beads, and a back plate with a brooch fastening, which is secured over the front part by folding the claws over it with pliers.

YOU WILL NEED

- **Sieve brooch finding**
- **Thread**
- **Needle**
- **Selection of brightly coloured beads**
- **Superglue**
- **Pliers**

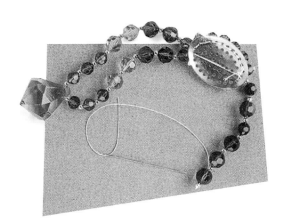

Thread a needle, then knot the thread to one side of the sieve. Thread on the beads to create a string the desired length. Take the needle and thread back through the sieve and secure on the wrong side, creating a bead loop. Repeat for the other side, varying the beads used. "Sew" smaller beads to the top by weaving the thread through the sieve, then the beads, and back through the sieve and up again for the next bead.

Add a single long string of beads to the centre front point and continue to build up your design, "sewing" the beads in the required position.

3 Dab a blob of glue on each point where the thread is secured or knotted. Place the back plate over the threads on the wrong side of the sieve and use pliers to fold over the claws that keep it in place.

PEARL CHAIN AND EARRINGS

This is a simple way to use readymade pearl chain with an effective result. We have added very dramatic ear-rings to go with the simplicity of the chain.

YOU WILL NEED

For the chain:
- **Ready-made pearl chain with 80 beads**
- **10 x 8 mm ($^{1}/_{3}$ in) pearl beads**
- **4 x 6 mm ($^{1}/_{4}$ in) pearl beads**
- **4 x pearl oval beads**
- **14 x 6 mm ($^{1}/_{4}$ in) metallized plastic rose beads**
- **8 x 3 mm ($^{1}/_{8}$ in) silver-plated balls**
- **10 x 50 mm (2 in) eyepins**
- **2 x 25 mm (1 in) eyepins**

For the ear-rings:
- **20 x 8 mm ($^{1}/_{3}$ in) pearl beads**
- **32 x 3 mm ($^{1}/_{8}$ in) silver-plated balls**
- **8 x 0/7 white rocailles**
- **50mm (2 in) chain**
- **8 x 25 mm (1 in) headpins**
- **2 x 38 mm (1$^{1}/_{2}$ in) eyepins**
- **1 pair earwires**

Tools:
- **Round-nosed pliers**
- **Wirecutters**

1 Cut the pearl chain into eight lengths, each of which has 10 of the little pearls on it. Thread the patterns for the straight pieces onto your 50 mm eyepins and roll the tops. We have made four the same and two with different patterns.

2 Gently open the loops on the eyepins to hook in the pieces of chain.

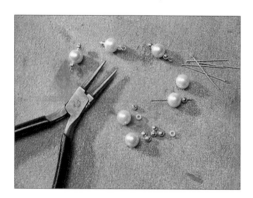

3 For the ear-rings, start by making the pieces on the headpins which have a silver-plated ball on the end, a pearl and then either a white rocaille, or another silver-plated ball. Roll the tops of the headpins.

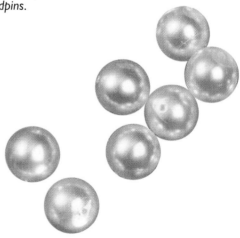

4 *Cut two 2.5 cm (1 in) pieces of chain
and hook the headpin pieces into them.*

5 *For the middle and the back of the chain
make linked pearl pieces. Two longer
straight pieces are linked onto a short
(25 mm) eyepin which has one pearl on it.*

6 Hang the chains from the bottom of the eyepins, put more pearl beads and silver-plated balls onto them, clip the ends and roll their tops. Attach the earwires to the top of these eyepins.

BEAD EMBROIDERY BRACELET

Decorative braids are usually used to trim fashion items or furnishing for the home, but here they have been completely transformed into unusual bracelets. Braid, ribbons, and even fancy cords can all be jazzed up and given a new purpose with simple bead embroidery. For a subtle, sophisticated look, choose a design that highlights the pattern or shape of the braid; or to create really impressive bracelets, completely cover the ribbon or braid with a collection of different ornate beads, buttons, or a combination of both.

YOU WILL NEED

- **A length of braid**
- **Beads**
- **Tailor's chalk**
- **Sewing needle**
- **Sewing thread or invisible thread**
- **Seed beads**

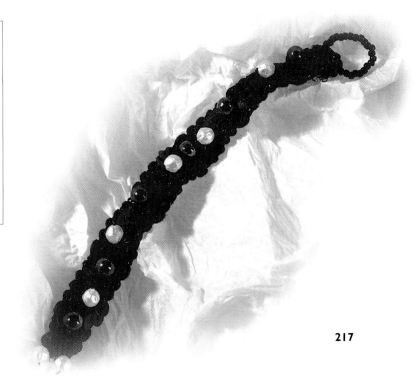

217

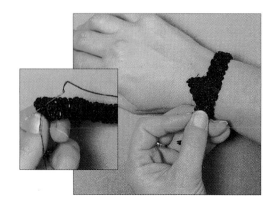

Use invisible thread or sewing thread that matches the beads and braid you are working with. The seed beads should be in colours that coordinate with the other materials as well.

1 *Cut a length of braid long enough to fit around your wrist, plus enough for turnings. Oversew or glue raw ends to neaten.*

Design Tips

- *Watch for interesting antique braids at yard sales and consignment shops – they can be found as decoration on anything from cushions to hats.*
- *Choose colours that will coordinate with a favourite outfit for a special occasion.*
- *Experiment with different widths of braid to create different effects.*
- *Choosing the right size, style, or colour of beads is essential to creating the right finished look – a hematite and pearl braid, for example, is perfect for a sophisticated bracelet to go with evening wear.*
- *The bead combination used for the braid project here would also look stylish on a black velvet bracelet. For a summer look, try adding a collection of mother-of-pearl buttons to a cream or white velvet band.*

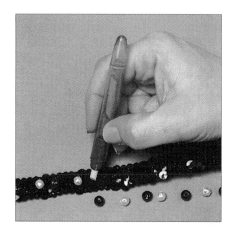

2 *Lay the braid out on a flat surface and work out your design. Use tailor's chalk to mark the required position for each bead.*

3 Sew each bead in place individually, making sure it is secure.

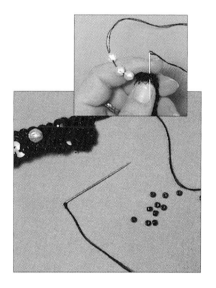

4 Join a double thread to the centre of an end. String on 3 beads that match those used to work the design, then fasten off the thread close to the start position so that the beads form a "tab". At the opposite end, join a double thread to the centre and thread on enough seed beads to make a loop that will slip neatly over the "tab" to join the two sides of the braid together.

ROCAILLE BEAD CHOKER

Tiny glass rocaille beads are often used in bead embroidery with bugle beads and sequins, but they also look fabulous strung into necklaces in a wide range of colours or worked in subtle colour combinations to match a favourite outfit. For this rope choker, the beads are threaded onto fine silk threads that are then twisted around each other to create the rope style. Threading on all the beads for each strand takes a little patience but the finished design is worth the effort. The more strands you make, the more lavish the necklace will look. Twisting the strands together to form a "rope" is a classic jewellery design often worked in pearls, but there are many variations on this style. Experiment by twisting the strands in groups and then all together, and try loosely braiding groups of strands for another look.

YOU WILL NEED
• **Tiny glass beads in 3 different colours**
• **Strong silk or invisible thread**
• **Beading needle**
• **8 Calotte crimps**
• **Pliers**
• **4 Jump rings**
• **2 Head pins**
• **2 Bell caps**
• **Wire cutters**
• **Necklace clasp**

This necklace is made up of 4 groups of bead strands, with 3 bead strands in each group. Work 2 of these groups in the same colour, and the other 2 in different, coordinating colours. Use a beading needle to thread several of the smaller beads onto the needle at once. Cut the thread into choker length, about 31 cm (12 in) without the clasp, plus 2.5 cm (1 in) to allow for twisting and another 31 cm (12 in) for easy threading and knotting.

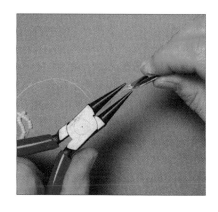

1 *Tie one end of a strand to a large stopper bead to prevent beads falling off while you work and thread on beads to the desired length. Tie the free end of the thread to a stopper bead and work another 2 strands to make up the group.*

2 *Untie the stopper beads and knot the 3 threads together. Slip the knot into a side-opening calotte, using pliers to close and secure the thread. At the other end, knot the threads together close to the last beads and secure with a calotte. Repeat for all strands.*

3 *Using pliers, open up a tiny jump ring, slip it through the loops of all the calottes at one end, and close to secure. Repeat for the opposite end.*

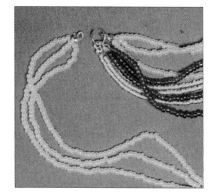

Design Tips

- *It is essential to work in good light when stringing very small beads.*

- *Delicate beads look best strung on a strong silk thread or invisible thread – anything heavier will spoil the effect.*

- *Add the occasional large bead to a strand to give the necklace a different scale.*

- *The more bead strands used to make up the choker, the more luxurious the finished look.*

- *Instead of twisting the strands around each other, make them long enough to tie into a central knot.*

- *For a central focus point, make a coordinating bead from Fimo or papier-mâché with a hole large enough to take all of the strands.*

- *Look for and use unusual necklace clasps or recycled ones from broken necklaces.*

4 Use pliers to turn a loop at one end of a head pin, slipping it through the jump ring before closing securely. Push the free end of the head pin through a bell cap hole. Pull it as far as it will go so that calottes and jump ring are covered. Trim the wire and turn another loop.

5 Open up a jump ring and insert through the loop on the bell cap and through the loop on one part of the necklace clasp. Close securely using pliers.

223

'JET' CHOKER

These faceted glass beads have been designed to look like jet beads, so we have designed a choker that could have come from a Jane Austen novel with them. It is made with simple free-hand weaving.

YOU WILL NEED

- **75 x 8 mm (¹/₃ in) 'jet' beads**
- **60 x 6 mm (¹/₄ in) 'jet' beads**
- **4 x 5 mm (¹/₄ in) 'jet' beads**
- **32 x 0/7 black rocailles**
- **2 calottes**
- **Polyester thread**
- **Chain**
- **Hook**

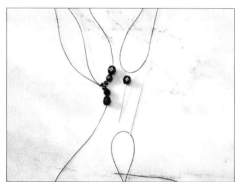

1 Cut 2 x 150 cm (5 ft) of thread; this is a generous amount, but will save the risk of running out of thread.

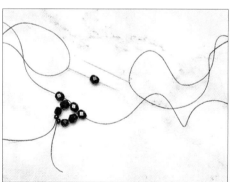

2 Use two needles with it. Knot the ends of the threads together. Put a rocaille, a 5 mm bead and a 6 mm bead onto each.

3 After five central beads, put a rocaille, a 6 mm ($^1/_4$ in) bead and another rocaille onto your bottom thread. Thread back up through the 6 mm ($^1/_4$ in) bead and the top rocaille, leaving the bottom one to hold the hanging beads.

4 Continue to weave, adding more hanging beads, and starting to use the larger (8 mm/$^1/_4$ in) beads. Return to the smaller beads towards the other end of the choker, so both ends match.

5 At the end of the choker make sure that the threads are pulled securely through, so that there are no gaps in the weaving, then knot the together. Put a calotte over the knots at both ends.

6 *Cut a small piece of chain for each end and open a link in the chain to attach it to the calotte. Add your hook to one side (this can be put into the chain at different lengths so that you can wear the choker in different ways).*

'JET' CHOKER

Variation on a Theme

Beads made from real jet are expensive, but such good glass and plastic imitations are available that you can make dramatic jewellery at an affordable price.

YOU WILL NEED

- **Black silk thread**
- **Pliers**
- **Scissors**
- **Rocaille**
- **Selection of 'jet' beads (graded in size)**
- **Clasp**
- **Calottes**

String beads on strands of black silk thread to make necklaces, and give them an authentic Victorian look by knotting the thread between each bead. The knots must be large enough not to slip through the bead holes, so add more strands of thread if necessary.

For a necklace with a fun tassel, first make up the basic necklace. Cut several strands of thread to one and one-half times the desired finished length (allowing for knots). make a practice knot to check that it will be large enough.

Start the necklace with a knot, then string on a bead and make the next knot, keeping it as close to the bead as possible. Thread on an even number of beads to the desired length, then place a calotte over each end knot and use pliers to press its two end sides together, concealing the knot inside. Trim the excess threads. Attach the loop on each side of a necklace clasp to the calotte on each side with the aid of pliers. Alternatively, the threads can be knotted to the loop on the clasp and then taken back through the beads to conceal them.

To make the tassel, shown here, thread small beads onto as many strands of thread as you wish. For each strand, take one end of a thread through a rocaille to act as a stopper, then take both ends of the thread through each additional bead. When you have enough strands, take all the thread ends through a large bead and secure with a knot. Knot the tassel between two beads at the centre front of the necklace, and take the thread ends back through the large bead to conceal them.

AMBER NECKLACE AND EARRINGS

Beautiful chunks of Baltic amber are threaded with plain chunky silver beads and ornate bead caps as a centre piece. The amber is so lovely that it does not need to have much added to it.

Join the silk thread to the fastener with knots. Five knots were used here.

YOU WILL NEED

For the necklace:
- **9 oval amber beads**
- **10 round amber beads**
- **6 amber tube beads**
- **10 Indian silver beads**
- **2 bead caps**
- **2 silver discs**
- **1 silver fastener**
- **1 silver split ring**
- **Silk thread**

For the ear-rings:
- **2 x 50 mm (2 in) eyepins**
- **2 round amber beads**
- **2 amber tube beads**
- **2 Indian silver beads**
- **4 silver discs**
- **1 pair earwires**

Tools:
- **Needle**
- **Round-nosed pliers for the ear-rings**
- **Scissors**

2 Thread the beads onto the silk, using the bead caps on the central bead.

3 Join the split ring to the necklace using five knots as before.

4 The ear-rings are simply put onto the eyepins and the tops are rolled. The earwires are put into the top loop on the eyepins.

LOOPED LOOM CHOKER

This choker is dark and sophisticated, but is an easy start to using a beadloom.

YOU WILL NEED

- 1 g 0/8 purple rocailles
- 110 x 0/7 grey rocailles
- 3 x 5 mm (¹/₄ in) purple glass beads
- **Thin black polyester**
- **Thread**
- **Thick black polyester**
- **Beadloom**
- **Fine beading needle**
- **Scissors**
- **Masking tape (optional)**

1 Cut nine 80 cm (2 ft 7 in) lengths of the
thin polyester thread and position them
onto the loom. Both outside edges
should have two threads in one groove
of the loom to give a firmer edge. Attach
another long thin thread to one of the
outside warp threads, and work this in
and out of alternate warp threads to give
a neat beginning to the looming.

2 Start to work the beads onto the loom.
Pick up six beads with your needle and
hold them beneath the warp threads
making sure that they fit neatly between
each one. Pull the needle and thread
through the beads, still holding the beads
in place with your finger.

3 Thread your needle back through the
same row of beads, making sure that
your needle is above each of the warp
threads. Continue with your looming,
changing to grey beads initially after 10
rows and then after every five rows. Roll
the beadwork back towards you as you
work along the loom, keeping the work
tightly together. You will need to make
the choker about 23 cm (9 in) long.
Finish with a few rows of thread only as
at the beginning, and remove the choker
from the loom.

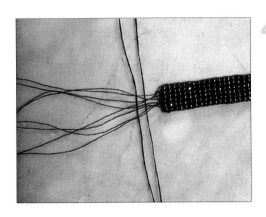

4 Cut two pieces of the thick thread 60 cm (2 ft) long for each end of the choker.

5 Plait on the new threads, using them together, and all the warp threads together. It helps to tape the choker to your work surface so that you can make the plaiting firm and close to the end of the looming.

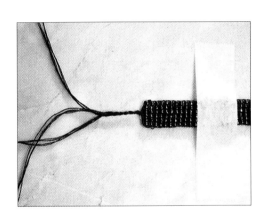

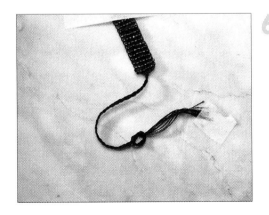

6 When your plaiting is long enough to tie the choker round your neck, knot all the ends together, and trim them neatly.

7 *If you have loose ends from joining new threads work these back into the choker with your needle.*

8 *Plait on the new threads, using them together, and all the warp threads together. It helps to tape the choker to your work surface so that you can make the plaiting firm and close to the end of the looming.*

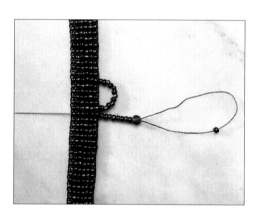

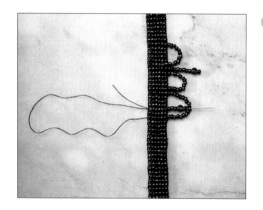

9 *When your plaiting is long enough to tie the choker round your neck, knot all the ends together, and trim them neatly.*

GLASS FANTASY NECKLACE AND EARRINGS

YOU WILL NEED

For the necklace:
- **9 assorted glass nuggets**
- **37 blue drops**
- **51 blue and green teardrops**
- **52 x 6 mm ('/₄ in) blue and green round glass beads**
- **18 x 0/8 rocailles in green or blue**
- **60 x 3 mm silver-plated balls**
- **2 cones**
- **4 x 38 mm (1 ¹/₂ in) eyepins**
- **10 crimps**
- **170 cm (5 ft 7 in) blue thread**
- **1 packet 0.8 silver-plated wire**

For the ear-rings:
- **2 matching nuggets**
- **1 pair earstuds + butterflies**

Tools:
- **Round-nosed pliers**
- **Necklace pliers**
- **Wirecutters**
- **Glue for ear-rings**

This is a lovely, over-the-top combination of beads, wire and glass nuggets. The nuggets are usually sold for display or flower arranging, but they combine beautifully with the rich blues and greens of the beads to make a really exotic necklace.

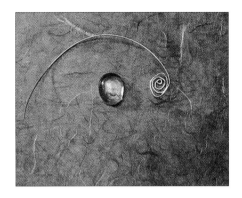

Start by working the wire round your glass nuggets. Cut a 25 cm (10 in) length of wire and make a coil at the beginning of it. Press a glass bauble into the coil so that it starts to enclose it.

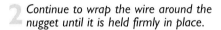

Continue to wrap the wire around the nugget until it is held firmly in place.

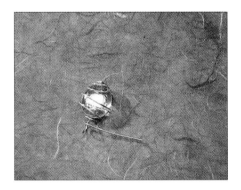

Make a loop above the nugget and coil the wire around the bottom of the loop, as shown in the techniques section. Trim off any excess wire. Wire the other nuggets in the same way.

Put four of the glass drops onto eyepins, roll the top to hang with the beads. Now plan out the design for the necklace on your threads. Cut three 40 cm (1 ft 4 in) lengths of thread, and work your beads, nuggets and drops onto the threads. Arrange them so that the colours and shapes are well balanced, and finish each of the threads with the rocailles which will go inside the cones.

5 *When you are happy with these threads crimp a neat loop at their ends. Cut two 15 cm (6 in) lengths of threads and make a loop with crimps at one end. Thread these through the loops at the ends of the main threads, and back into themselves. Then put your cones over the ends.*

6 *Thread the rest of the beads above the cones and finish by crimping on the fastener.*

7 *The studs are glued onto the back of the two nuggets to make matching ear-rings.*

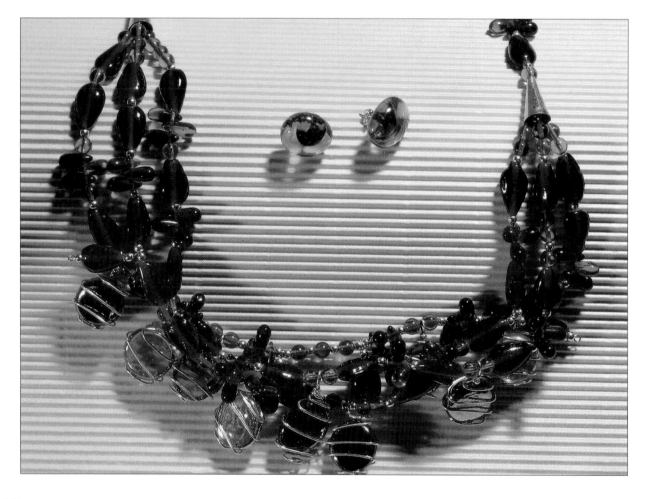

SPARKLING SEQUIN AND BEAD BRACELET

Sequins do not normally spring to mind when considering materials for making bracelets, but they can be made into quite spectacular and unusual designs. They are available in a variety of shapes, a kaleidoscopic range of colours, and are inexpensive, all of which makes them perfect for fun jewellery designs. Sequin motifs in the shape of flowers, leave, birds, and butterflies make fun charms suspended form a sequin or bead bracelet, while the classic smooth surface discs look stylish, especially if they have a hologram finish. You can mix them together in wild colour combinations or two-tone shades. Sequins that come with holes to one side are the easiest to use and can be made into instant charms, but other designs can be used too. They are all easy to pierce with the point of a needle.

YOU WILL NEED

• **Flower shaped sequins**
• **Rocaille beads**
• **Clear drying craft glue**
• **Toothpick**
• **Needle**
• **Jump rings**
• **Eye pins**
• **Round nosed pliers**
• **Wire cutters**
• **Nylon thread or tiger tail**
• **2 calotte crimps**
• **Gold rocaille beads**
• **Clasp**

You will need lots of tiny rocaille beads that colour coordinate with the flower-shaped sequins, as well as gold rocaille beads. The number of sequin charms that you use will vary depending on how close together you attach them.

Design Tips

- *Experiment with different charm designs, suspending them in a variety of ways.*
- *Attach a mixture of solid and open-centered oval sequins in a mix of colours.*
- *Craft and bead specialists often sell sequin sweepings that contain quite unusual shapes. These cost less than normal as they are literally swept up from where they fall during packing. They are cleaned and then bagged as an assortment.*
- *Use a fine needle to pierce a hole first, then enlarge it carefully if necessary with a thicker needle or by running the finer one around and around the hole – a large needle will shred some smaller sequins. A piece of cork under the sequin will make this process easier.*
- *Create pretty theme bracelets by stringing together associated sequin shapes, such as stars and moons, or birds, butterflies and flowers.*

Glue rocaille beads in shades of the same colour over the centre hole of each flower sequin that will be used as a charm. The number of charms needed will vary depending on how close together you attach them.

2 Use the point of a needle to make a small hole in a petal of each flower sequin to attach a jump ring. Twist the jump rings to open and insert them through the hole on each sequin that will be made into a charm.

3 Thread 3 or 4 gold rocailles onto an eye pin. Trim the pin with wire cutters so that approximately 1 cm (³⁄₈ in) extends beyond the beads. Turn this into a loop using the tips of pliers.

4 Measure and cut your chosen thread to fit around your wrist with room for knots, then knot the end and secure it to a calotte crimp. Thread on the sequins, taking the thread through the centre hole with gold beads spaced between each sequin, adding charms as you work.

5 When the bracelet reaches the right length, finish it off with another knot secured in a calotte crimp. Twist open 2 jump rings and attach them to each calotte crimp. Complete the bracelet by attaching a clasp to a jump ring.

TRIPLE PEARL AND BLACK ROCAILLE BEAD CHOKER AND EARRINGS

This necklace is simple to make but looks very sophisticated. It is worth buying a really beautiful clasp for it to set off the pearl beads and make the most of them.

YOU WILL NEED

For the necklace:
- 91 x 10 mm (¹/₂ in) pearls
- 100 x 0/7 black rocailles
- 6 french crimps
- 6 x 8 mm silver-plated balls
- 140 cm (4 ft 8 in) tiger tail clasp

For the ear-rings:
- 2 pearl cabochon
- 1 pair studs + butterflies

Tools:
- Necklace pliers
- Glue

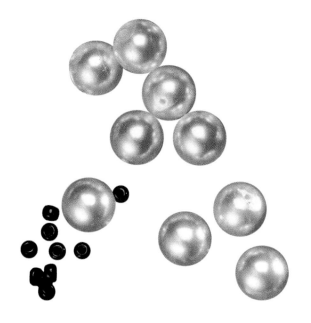

1 Thread the pearl beads onto 3 graduating lengths of the tiger tail, with a black rocaille between each bead. We have 28 pearl beads on the top row, 30 on the middle row and 33 on the bottom row.

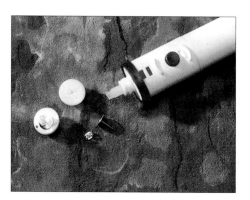

2 Finish each row with a rocaille, a silver-plated ball and another rocaille, and then crimp to the fastener and trim the ends of the tiger tail.

3 For the ear-rings, simply glue a stud to the back of the cabochon.

BELL-CAP AND BEAD EARRINGS

The filigree bell caps used to make these earrings are just one of the many decorative findings available and are multi-purpose, too. Here they are used to dangle bead strands, but they can also be used on both sides of a bead to make it look more special or to begin and end a necklace or bracelet. The ready-made holes around the edges are perfect for joining bead strands using a jump ring. The central hole can be wired with a longer strand and provide the link for an ear wire. This style of earring can be bold and striking or pretty and delicate, depending on the size of the bell cap and the beads used for the dangles.

YOU WILL NEED

- **2 filigree bell caps**
- **Beads**
- **Eye pins**
- **Wire cutters**
- **Pliers**
- **2 ear wires**
- **Jump rings**

Select beads in several shades of the same colour and in a few varied sizes. Remember that you don't have to thread bead strands through all of the holes on the filigree bell caps; this project uses only 4 strands per earring.

1 Thread the beads in groups or singularly onto an eye pin.

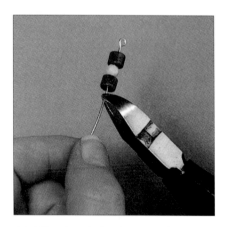

2 Trim the pin, leaving enough wire to turn another loop.

Design Tips

- *Sketch out design ideas on paper to experiment with different colour combinations and sizes and shapes of beads.*
- *It is important to get the strands to balance correctly or the earrings will look lopsided.*
- *Vary the number and length of the bead strands to create different effects.*
- *One single strand of large beads can look quite dramatic hung from the centre hole.*
- *Experiment with different styles and shapes of bell caps. Fluted bell caps conceal the connection between the top of the beaded strands, making it look like a beaded tassel.*

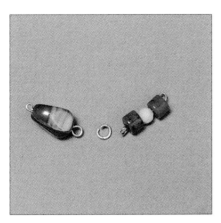

3 To make the strands, open up a
jump ring and slip through the loops
of 2 beaded pins. Close the ring
securely. Join as many beaded pins
together as necessary to get the
length required.

5 Before closing the ring, slip it
through the loop at the end of a
bead strand, then close securely.

4 Open up the jump rings and slip
through the holes around the end
of the bell cap.

6 Add as many strands as you wish to the edge of the bell cap, then insert an eye pin through the central hole so that the preformed loop sits on top of the cap. Trim the pin and turn a loop at the other end.

7 Join the central strand to the last loop with a jump ring. Close securely.

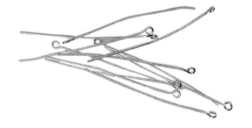

8 To complete the earrings, open up the loop at the bottom of an ear wire and slip through the central loop on the top of the bell cap. Close securely.

TRIANGLES NECKLACE AND EARRINGS

A striking combination of iridescent beads and angular shapes all worked together to produce a necklace that will allow you to make an entrance – anywhere.

YOU WILL NEED

For the necklace:
- 72 x ¹/₃ in (8 mm) blue faceted beads
- 107 x 0/7 grey rocailles
- 8 x blue triangle beads
- 2 calottes
- 1 fastener
- 4 m (10 ft) black polyester thread

For the ear-rings:
- 4 blue triangle beads
- 6 x 0/7 grey rocailles
- 2 x ¹/₃ in (8 mm) blue faceted beads
- 4 x 38 mm (1 ¹/₂ in) eyepins
- 1 pair earwires

Tools:
- Necklace pliers
- Round-nosed pliers for the ear-rings
- 2 fine needles

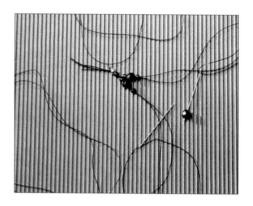

Cut two 150 cm (5 ft) lengths of thread and use them double with the fine needles. Knot the ends and put a calotte over the knot. Thread a rocaille onto both pairs of threads, separate the threads into the first faceted beads with rocailles either side of them. Bring all the threads into the next bead, working from both sides so that the threads cross in the centre of the bead.

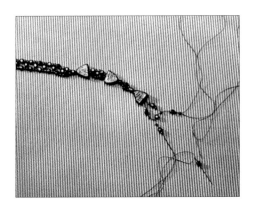

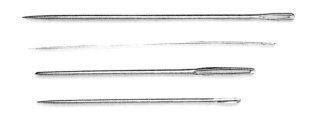

2 Continue to weave through the first section of beads, then bring both threads through a triangle bead. Now use triangles and weaving, changing the direction of the triangle beads as you work.

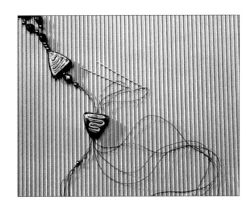

3 Bring both threads through the hanging beads, put a rocaille onto the bottom and thread back up through the beads above it, so that the rocaille holds the beads on the hanging piece.

4 Repeat your design on the other side of the choker. When you have finished check that the beads are neatly positioned on the threads, then knot again at this side and put another calotte over the knot. Add the fastener.

5 The loop on the top of the bottom eyepin on the ear-rings is linked into the bottom of the top eyepin, so that the ear-ring has extra movement.

PINK BEADS AND ANTIQUE GOLD NECKLACE AND EARRINGS

YOU WILL NEED

For the necklace:
- 26 x $^{1}/_{3}$ in (8 mm) pink beads
- 52 x $^{1}/_{4}$ in (6 mm) pink beads
- 2 antiqued gold triangles
- 1 antiqued gold ring
- 140 cm (4 ft 8 in) black thread
- 10 gilt french crimps
- 22 x $^{1}/_{8}$ in (3 mm) gold-plated balls
- 180 x 0/6 red rocailles
- 1 ornate fastener

For the ear-rings:
- 6 x 38 mm (1 $^{1}/_{2}$ in) eyepins
- 22 x 0/6 red rocailles
- 14 x $^{1}/_{8}$ in (3 mm) gold-plated balls
- 8 x $^{1}/_{3}$ in (8 mm) pink beads
- 6 x $^{1}/_{4}$ in (6 mm) pink beads
- 2 x antiqued gold triangles
- 1 pair earwires

Tools:
- **Round-nosed pliers for the ear-rings**
- **Necklace pliers**
- **Scissors**

As the name suggests, this is another really glitzy necklace. Both the rocailles and the round beads have an extra sheen and depth to their colour to add to the richness of the piece.

1 Cut three pieces of the thread, increasing in length between 30 and 35 cm (1 ft and 1 ft 2 in). Thread the ring into the middle of them and then arrange the pink beads and rocailles onto each of the threads.

2 When you have finished the arrangement, crimp the ends of the threads onto the triangles, putting a rocaille between the crimp and the triangle.

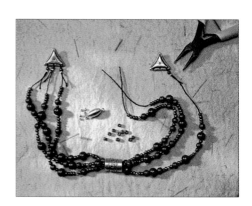

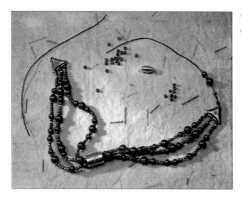

3 Cut two 15 cm (6 in) lengths of thread and crimp these to the tops of the triangles in the same arrangement as before, then thread the beads onto these threads. Attach the fastener with crimps, again putting a rocaille between the fastener and the crimps at each end.

4 Make the hanging pieces for the ear-rings by threading the eyepins and rolling their tops. Then open these loops sideways to hang the pieces from the triangles. Put the earwire into the top of the triangle.

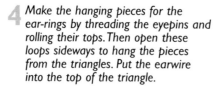

5.2

CLASSIC CHIC
BEAD DECORATION

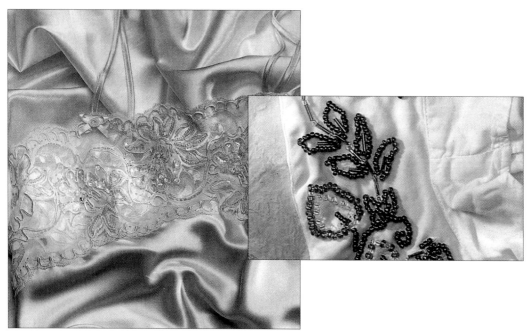

Classic jewels can also be used to add an individual look to clothing, accessories or even household items.

The projects which follow are simple to do and will inspire you to come up with your own ideas and designs.

EMBROIDERED BLOUSE

Here we let the design on the item suggest the project to us! You could draw a design onto the garment and then embroider the beads onto that, as we have shown on our sample piece. Or you can choose something like the blouse illustrated, which already had a design on it.

YOU WILL NEED

- **Blouse (patterned or unpatterned)**
- **Pattern (if using unpatterned blouse)**
- **Selection of beads**
- **Beading needle**
- **Invisible thread**

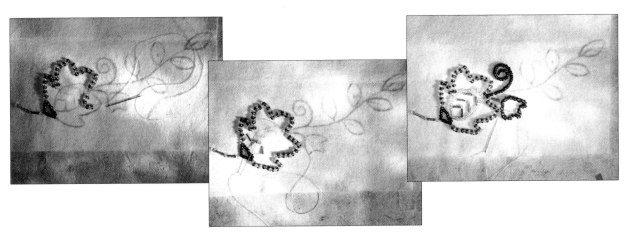

You could sew on individual beads using a backstitch. Or you can work small sections by threading a few beads onto your pattern, and then bring your thread back through the other side and catch your beaded thread, to stop the beads having too much movement.

If you were doing a very beautiful piece of bead embroidery, you could use couching. To do this you have your beads on one thread, and use another thread to come from below between each bead to secure them. Don't forget to only use beads that can be washed if you are embroidering with them.

EMBROIDERED CAMISOLE
Variation on a Theme

Bold and bedazzling, there is nothing understated about this eye-catching top. The rich jewel colours embroidered on to sophisticated cream satin create a sizzling effect that is just right for parties.

Lay out the camisole on a flat surface and place the beads on top, working out your design before stitching them into position. Create a bright and jazzy top by using colours together, as shown here, or achieve a softer effect with one or two colours in less vibrant shades.

<table>
<tr><td>

YOU WILL NEED

- **Camisole**
- **Selection of flat backed stones**
- **Invisible thread**
- **Beading needle**

</td></tr>
</table>

The flat-backed stones have a hole on either side, just above the base, and are easy to sew on. Using a fine invisible thread and a beading needle, bring the thread up from the wrong side, take it through the holes in the stone and back through to the wrong side, pulling the thread firmly to keep the stone in place. Bring the thread back up, close to the next stone and continue working in the same way. Depending on the type of fabric and the ornateness of the design, you may find it easier to apply a lightweight iron-on interfacing to the wrong side of the fabric to give a firmer backing and to prevent the weight of the beads from dragging it down.

EMBROIDERED CAMISOLE

Variation on a Theme

Choose a camisole that has three or four large flower motifs rather than several small ones, which will be difficult to work and will look less effective.

Take a length of thread, not too long, tie a knot in the end and make a small stitch on the wrong side of the camisole. Take the thread through to the front.

Pick up four pearl beads and lay them flat against the material, curving them slightly to form part of a circle. Take the needle through to the back, bring it through to the front between the second and third beads. Take the thread through the two beads and pick up two more beads. Continue to work in this way to complete the circle.

YOU WILL NEED

- **Approximately 500 x 2.5 mm (1 in) pearls**
- **3 gm (¹/₈ oz) 5mm (¹/₄ in) sequins**
- **8 small crystal drops with top holes**
- **3 gm (¹/₈ oz) transparent rocaille beads, size 1 2/0 (optional)**
- **Unwaxed beading thread**
- **Camisole with lace top**
- **Scissors**
- **Beading needle**

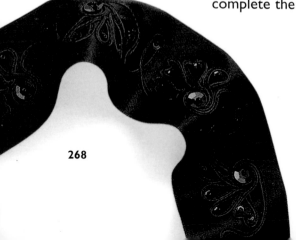

Sequins and rocailles in a darker shade add a dramatic touch.

Outline one side of the leaf or petal shapes with pearl beads, curving the line gently. Do not add too many beads or their weight will pull the garment out of shape.

With a new length of thread, attach sequins to the other petals. Bring the thread through to the right side, pick up a sequin, cup-side facing upwards, then the thread through to the wrong side

near to the edge of the sequin. Bring the thread through to the right side close to your previous stitch and pick up a second sequin, which will overlap the first sequin. Continue to add lines of sequins in this way.

Finally, sew two crystal drops to the middle of the pearl circles. Take your thread through each bead twice to make sure that it is held firmly.

Some of the sequins can be attached with rocailles. Bring your thread through to the right side, pick up a sequin, cup-shaped side up, pick up the rocaille and take you thread back through the sequin so that the rocaille holds the sequin in place. If you use this method, the edges of the sequin should just touch, not overlap.

EMBROIDERED HAT

Variation on a Theme

B eautiful fabrics and an eclectic mix of tiny beads, sequins, found objects and embroidery materials have been combined to produce a unique piece of clothing.

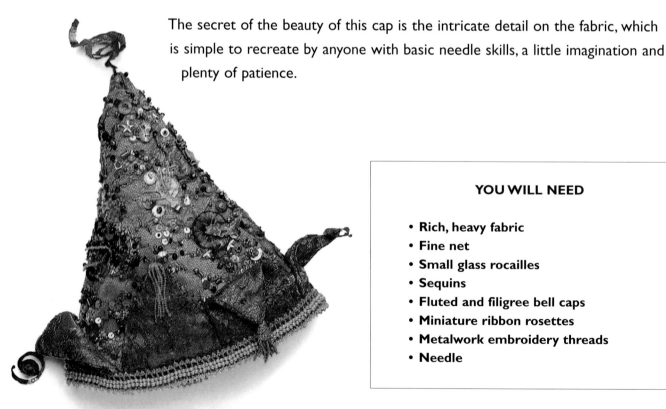

The secret of the beauty of this cap is the intricate detail on the fabric, which is simple to recreate by anyone with basic needle skills, a little imagination and plenty of patience.

YOU WILL NEED

- **Rich, heavy fabric**
- **Fine net**
- **Small glass rocailles**
- **Sequins**
- **Fluted and filigree bell caps**
- **Miniature ribbon rosettes**
- **Metalwork embroidery threads**
- **Needle**

The same technique can be used to make this spectacular waistcoat.

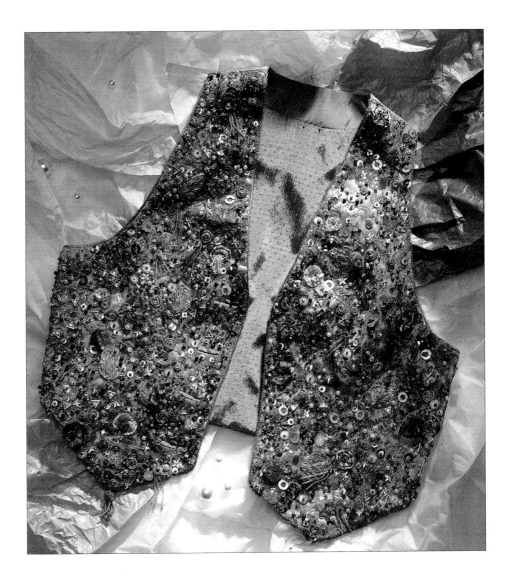

Use a rich heavy brocade for the front fabric, and top this with a layer of fine net. Cover this densely with tiny sequins and glass rocailles and metalwork embroidery threads. Add interest by using small fluted and filigree bell caps secured with tiny beads and miniature ribbon rosettes to highlight larger beads.

Work the main embroidery before making up the lining. Oversew the edges to prevent fraying while you work and remember not to work too close to seams if you plan to machine stitch the pieces together or to add a rich corded edge. You can add detail after making up the main piece, taking care to stitch through the top layer of fabric only.

EVENING BAG

This project will require time and patience, but your effort will be rewarded. The bag is made in strips on a beadloom, then lined with felt and finished with cords. It is big enough to carry your keys and some money for a glamourous night out.

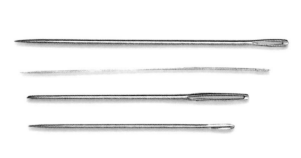

YOU WILL NEED

- **90 g (3 oz) 0/7 iridescent blue rocailles**
- **20 g (³/₄ oz) 0/7 iridescent clear rocailles**
- **10 g (³/₈ oz) 0/7 light blue rocailles**
- **A piece of black felt 10 x 20 cm (4 x 8 in)**
- **1.5 m (5 ft) black cord**
- **Beadloom**
- **Beading needle**
- **Scissors**
- **Glue**
- **Needle**

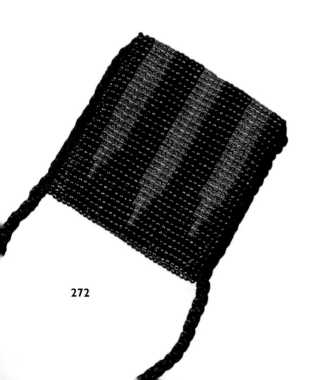

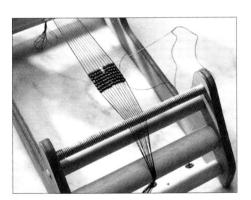

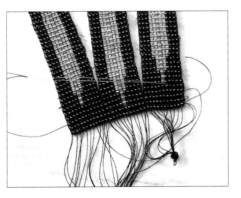

1 Set up the beadloom as shown in the techniques section. There are 11 rocailles in each strip. You will need three strips and there are 57 rows in each strip. Remember to introduce the colour changes differently on the central strip.

2 When the three strips are complete, work the loose threads at the sides of the strips back into the weaving. Then connect the strips together by running a thread through all of the pieces.

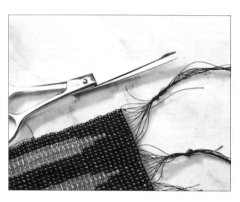

3 Knot the warp threads together and trim them.

5 Sew neatly along all the edges so that the felt and the beading cannot separate.

4 Glue the piece of felt to the beading, making sure that all the loose ends of threads are trapped between the two.

6 Fold the piece in half and sew the cord down the sides, making sure that you have the bottom of the cord neatly tucked under.

EVENING BAG

Variation on a Theme

The quilted design on the bag shown provided the inspiration for the geometric pattern. Brilliant coloured "lozenge"-shaped beads emphasise the quilting and glisten beautifully when they catch the light.

YOU WILL NEED

- **Fabric bag**
- **Strong cotton thread**
- **Beading needle**
- **Selection of brightly coloured beads**
- **1.5 m (5 ft) black cord**

The slightly flattened shape of these beads lends itself to this type of decoration, as they will not catch on other objects. Large, rounded beads would create more of a problem, although small beads would look effective and could be used in greater quantities.

Fabric bags are ideal for decorating in this way, as it is easy to stitch the beads in place. A leather bag is more difficult to work but if you use a

fine leather needle with its specially shaped point you can be just as creative, using beads as a trim on a bag or in an overall design.

Use a strong cotton thread and fasten it securely on the inside of the bag where it will not be seen. Bring the needle through to the right side at the point at which the bead is to be attached and take it through the bead and back through to the inside. Repeat this several times to secure the bead, as you would a button and fasten off the thread on the inside.

EVENING BAG
Variation on a Theme

S titching beads on a plain evening bag is an easy way of adding sparkle and glamour. Small beads at the end of the drawstring make for a festive touch.

Use a tape measure and pins or chalk pencil to mark a row of triangles around the base of the bag. Next, take a length of thread and tie a knot in the end. Take the thread through from the inside of the bag to the bottom of one of the triangles around the base.

Pick up approximately eight green bugles, then take the needle through the apex of the triangle and pull the thread until the beads are lying flat against the fabric. Taking the needle through the inside of the bag each time, secure the row of bugles in place by making a tiny

YOU WILL NEED

- **10 gm ($^1/_2$ oz) 0/7 green bugles**
- **10 gm ($^1/_2$ oz) 0/7 green rocaille beads size 12/0**
- **7 x 5 mm ($^1/_4$ in) amber facet beads**
- **7 x 3 mm ($^1/_8$ in) transparent facet beads**
- **15 red rocaille beads, size 8/0**
- **6 x 8 mm ($^1/_3$ in) green facet beads**
- **Assorted small facet beads**
- **Beading thread to match colour of bag**
- **Soft evening bag in plain colour**
- **Tape measure**
- **Dressmaking pins or dressmaker's chalk pencil**
- **Scissors**
- **Beading needle**

stitch between each bead to hold the thread down. Finish off the thread neatly and securely at the end of the row, on the inside of the bag. Repeat until you have completed the sides of all triangles.

Using green bugles and the same technique, add the row of beads all around the base of the bag. Using a new length of thread with a knot in the end, bring your needle through from the inside of the bag and begin to add the green rocailles in a random pattern inside each of the triangles. Stitch each rocaille in position individually and use about 20 in each triangle. Finish

off the thread securely after completing each triangle. Use a new length of thread to attach an amber and a clear bead and a red rocaille to the apex of each triangle. Finish off the thread securely each time. Stitch green rocaille beads around the top of the bag, placing them about 5mm ($^1/_4$ in) apart. Using individual lengths of thread, attach a large green bead and a red rocaille to the tip of the triangular points around the top of the bag. Take the thread up through the green bead and the rocaille, then down through the green bead only.

If your bag has a drawstring, add some matching faceted beads and rocailles to the ends of the tassels and secure with knots.

GLOBAL INSPIRATION

As society becomes more multicultural, fashion follows suit. New technology such as the internet and satellite television, enables us to see far and away places without even needing to travel!

The projects in this section take inspiration from materials, patterns and colours used in clothing and jewellery abroad and adapt them to create some exciting pieces.

LAPIS LAZULI NECKLACE

This necklace is a wonderful combination of chips of Chinese turquoise, large lapis lazuli beads from Afghanistan, old coral from Nepal, and tiny silver beads from Thailand. It is completed with a Balinese clasp. A necklace for dreaming of faraway travels!

YOU WILL NEED

- 1 x 90 cm (3 ft) string of Chinese turquoise chips
- 1 large lapis lazuli bead
- 4 x 8 mm ($^1/_3$ in) lapis lazuli beads
- 4 coral chunks
- 14 x 7 mm ($^1/_4$ in) Thai silver beads
- 3 cards of No. 5 black silk thread
- 2 calottes
- Balinese hook fastener and jump ring
- Necklace pliers
- Scissors
- Fishing line to plan the necklace on

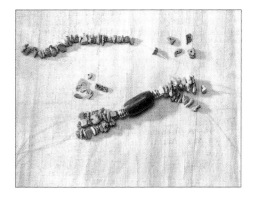

The chips of turquoise cannot be counted to get even lengths, and the odd sizes need to be balanced around the necklace, so it makes sense with this necklace to plan it on fishing line.

2 *You can also reject any damaged chips or ones that sit badly at this stage.*

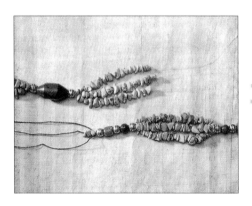

3 *Unwind the silk thread on your cards and knot the ends together. Put some glue onto the knot and then put a calotte over the knot. Rethread your necklace onto the silk, working each section back toward the calotte as you thread.*

4 *Finish with another knot and calotte as before. Attach the hook and the jump ring to the calottes.*

INDIAN SILK AND BEAD EARRINGS AND BROOCH

This exquisite gilt-edged brooch and earrings borrow from the colours, materials and contrasting textures used in traditional Indian textiles. The fabric is decorated with rich machine embroidery then embellished with handsewn tiny beads.

YOU WILL NEED

- **Piece of silk fabric at least 10 cm x 20 cm (4 in x 8 in)**
- **Craft-weight interfacing**
- **Sewing machine**
- **Selection of machine embroidery threads including a gold metallic and a shaded thread**
- **Selection of small beads**
- **No 2 round cane**
- **1 large bead**
- **Needle**
- **Fine copper wire**
- **Pliers**
- **Thin card**
- **Bondaweb**
- **Brooch back**
- **Ear wires**
- **2 tiny shells**

1 Cut two pieces or silk fabric and one piece of craft-weight interfacing each about 12 mm (¹/₂ in) bigger than the finished brooch, which will be 7.5 cm (3 in) square. Sandwich them together, then set your sewing machine to straight stitch and outline the shape of the brooch and an inner square. The outlines can be drawn in pencil or chalk prior to stitching, if necessary.

2 To create the gold outlines, first wind the metallic thread on to the bobbin, bypassing the tension mechanism by taking the thread through the hole in the bobbin case. Thread the top of the machine with a shaded thread. Using straight stitch and working on the back of the brooch, sew several lines around the inner square (the design will come out on the front of the brooch)

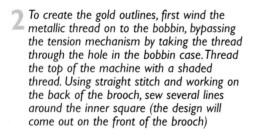

288

3 The star motif is "drawn" with free machine embroidery, for which you have to drop or cover the feed dog, according to the machine handbook. This allows the fabric to move freely, enabling you to "draw" with the machine. Replace the normal sewing foot with a darning foot, thread with your chosen colour and slacken the top tension. Stitch the outline of the star shape then fill it in, shading with a different colour if required.

4 Trim the fabric to within 2mm ($^1/_{12}$ in) of the outer stitching. Return the machine to normal stitching and, using a close zigzag stitch, sew over the raw edges for a neat finish. More open zigzag stitches in a different colour add interest. Neaten the thread ends.

5 Decorate the outer edge with small beads handsewn in place. Overstitch pieces of cane in position to outline the inner square and star motif, adding more beads as decorative detail. The large bead at the bottom of the brooch is attached with fine copper wire twisted into a loop with pliers then joined to one of the small beads already stitched to the outer edge.

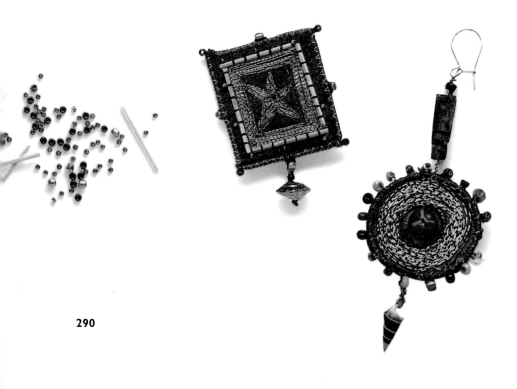

6 To stiffen the brooch, cut a piece of card and a piece of Bondaweb to the correct size then cut a piece of fabric 6 mm ($^1/_4$ in) bigger than these. Place the Bondaweb on top of the card then centre the fabric on top of this. Fold the fabric around the card then iron to fix, following the manufacturer's instructions. Sew the brooch back in place, then oversew the completed backing to the brooch to finish.

7 The earrings are made using the same techniques. Attach the ear wires and shells with twisted wire.

291

KNOTTED CHINESE NECKLACE AND EARRINGS

These lovely Chinese porcelain beads have been combined with little enamelled bead caps to highlight their colours. We have used a thick thread and knotted between the beads, so that you can learn how to know while you make a beautiful necklace.

YOU WILL NEED

For the necklace:
- **26 x 15 mm ($^1/_2$ in) Chinese porcelain beads**
- **52 x 8 mm ($^1/_3$ in) bead caps**
- **1 m (3 ft) thick blue thread**
- **2 calottes**
- **Fastener**

For the ear-rings:
- **2 x 50 mm (2 in) eyepins**
- **2 x 15 mm ($^1/_2$ in) Chinese porcelain beads**
- **10 x 8 mm ($^1/_8$ in) s.p.balls**
- **2 x 6 mm ($^1/_4$ in) metallized plastic beads**
- **1 pair earstuds with loop and butterfly**

Tools:
- **Necklace pliers**
- **Strong needle**

Knot your thread and put calotte over the knot.

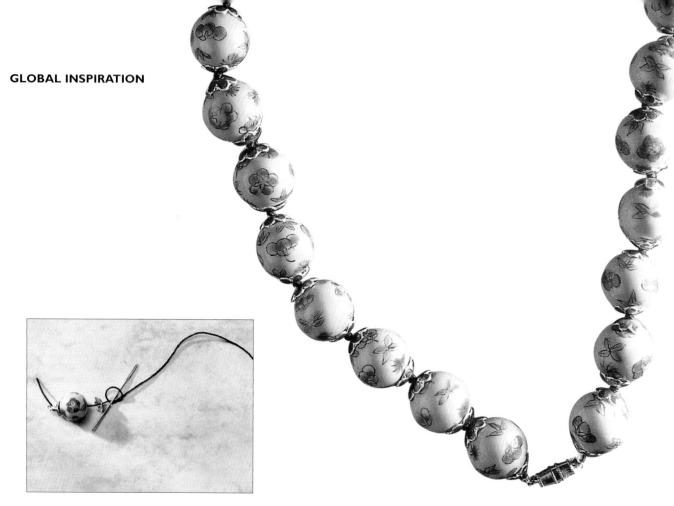

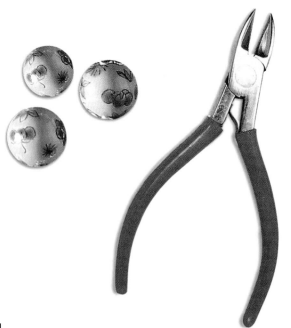

2 *Thread the first bead with the bead caps either side of it and make a knot after the bead (the knot is shown in the techniques section).*

3 *Continue to add the beads and bead caps and the knot between each bead. Finish with a knot after the last bead. Put another calotte on the knot.*

4 *Attach the fastener to your calottes.*

5 *The ear-rings are simply threaded onto the eyepins with a rolled top.*

MILLEFIORI BEAD NECKLACE

Millefiori beads were originally made from glass by the Venetians and were highly sought after all over the world. Translated, "Millefiori" means "a thousand flowers" because the Venetians could get so many slices of the same flower from one glass cane. Today, the same basic techniques can be applied to polymer clays to create spectacular beads like the ones shown here. Different coloured clays in striking combinations are rolled and wrapped around each other to make the "millefiori cane". This is carefully and gently rolled to form a much narrower cane from which fine slices are cut and used to cover a plain base bead. The technique is not as difficult to master as it may seem and the cane can be used to make amazing jewellery on its own.

YOU WILL NEED

For the millefiori cane:
- **Fimo in 4 different colours**
- **Rolling pin**
- **Craft knife**

For the base beads:
- **Fimo in other colours to go with the cane**
- **Wooden skewer**
- **Varnish**

For the necklace:
- **Nylon thread**
- **2 calotte crimps**
- **Sewing needle**
- **Small spacer beads**
- **Necklace clasp**
- **Pliers**

Decorations for these beads are sliced from a tube of "cane" made of 7 logs of clay wrapped together. Knead the Fimo with your thumbs and fingers until really soft and pliable, to prevent cracks and to make it much easier to roll. Wash your hands when changing colours to prevent one hue rubbing off on another. Cut the nylon thread to a length of 61 cm (24 in) plus 15 cm (6 in) for knotting.

1 To make the centre of the cane, use the palms of your hands to roll out a log from 1 colour of Fimo approximately 6 mm (¹/₄ in) in diameter.

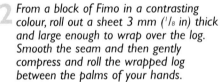

2 From a block of Fimo in a contrasting colour, roll out a sheet 3 mm (¹/₈ in) thick and large enough to wrap over the log. Smooth the seam and then gently compress and roll the wrapped log between the palms of your hands.

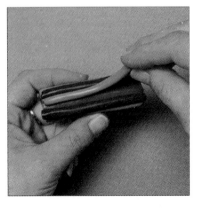

3 Roll out 3 logs of equal diameter from each of the remaining colours, and build the cane by alternating the logs around the centre, as shown. Gently compress together and roll between the palms of your hands.

Design Tips

- A book on the history of beads or even old pieces of jewellery can provide inspiration for millefiori designs.

- Sketch designs on paper and colour with felt-tip pens or paints that match the colours of the clays.

- Cut out wedges of clay and substitute for or alternate with logs to get another style of design.

- Experiment with base beads in different shapes – tubes, square, cylinders, and ovals are all easy to mould in your hands.

- Heavy clay beads need to be strung on a strong thread like nylon, but if you prefer to use a cotton or silk in a matching colour use 4 to 6 strands together and knot the thread between each bead.

- Use beads in brilliant contrasting colours or simple combinations like black and white.

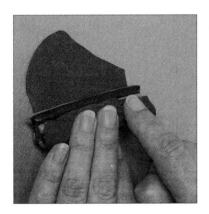

4 Roll out another sheet of Fimo in one of the colours used for the centre and wrap around the cane. Smooth the seam and gently compress together. You may find it easier to cut the cane into shorter lengths before wrapping with the last sheet of Fimo.

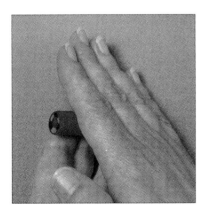

5 Roll the cane carefully and evenly between the palms of your hands first, then on a flat surface until the diameter is about 6 mm ($^1/_4$ in).

6 To make base beads, roll them into balls or tubes. Cut off the misshapen end of the cane, then cut the rest into thin slices. Cover each bead with millefiori slices and roll gently in your palms to merge them together.

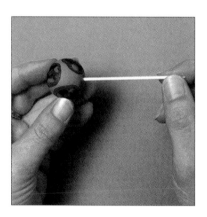

7 Leave the beads for several hours. Pierce a central hole in each using a wooden skewer or knitting needle. Bake in a low temperature oven following instructions. Apply a coat of varnish to bring out all the colours. Let dry for 24 hours before threading the beads.

8 Cut the nylon thread to the length required, make a large knot in one end, and take the other end through a calotte. With the knot sitting neatly in the cup of the calotte, use pliers to secure the thread. String the beads on in the order you want, placing small spacer beads between each clay bead. Knot the remaining end of thread close to the last bead and secure to a calotte. Attach necklace clasp to loops on each calotte, closing the loops with pliers to secure.

THAI SILVER NECKLACE

A simple but stunning arrangement of silver beads from Thailand. The beads are made using the traditional skills of the Khymer craftsmen, who have come over the borders from Cambodia.

YOU WILL NEED

For the necklace:
- 13 large silver beads
- 14 medium silver beads
- 6 small ribbed silver beads
- 34 small plain silver beads
- 4 tiny silver beads
- 1 trigger catch
- 1 jump ring
- Grey silk thread

For the ear-rings:
- 2 large silver beads
- 2 medium silver beads
- 2 small plain silver beads
- 2 tiny silver beads
- 2 x 50 mm (2 in) eyepins
- 1 pair earwires

Tools:
- Scissors
- Needle
- Round-nosed pliers

1 *Start by knotting your thread onto the fastener. There are four knots between the first bead and the fastener.*

2 *Thread your beads. As these beads are handmade they are slightly different shapes and sizes, and you should arrange them so they sit well together.*

3 *Finish by knotting on to the jump ring at the other side of the necklace.*

4 *The ear-rings are simple straight ear-rings with rolled tops.*

CERAMIC BEAD NECKLACE

Earthy-coloured ceramic beads are widely spaced on a linen thread to create a simple, natural effect.

YOU WILL NEED

- Scissors
- 2.30 m (2.5 yards) of thick linen thread ruler
- 12 natural ceramic bead

I Cut two lengths of linen thread, 115 cm (45 in) each. Tie one end of each length in a knot, approximately 6 cm (2.5 in) from the end of each piece of thread.

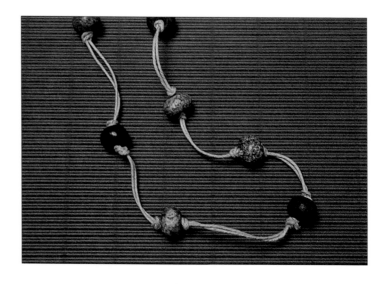

2 Slide a ceramic bead onto the threads until it rests on the knot. Tie another on the other side of the ceramic bead, securing it in place. Measure 5 cm (2 in) from the bead and tie another knot. Slide on another bead and secure this with a knot. Repeat this process until all the beads are used.

3 To finish the necklace, tie the ends of the threads together next to a bead so that the fastening is discreetly covered.

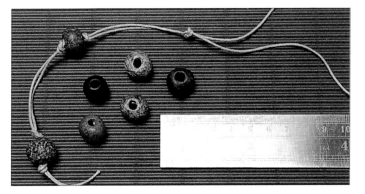

INCA CHOKER AND EARRINGS

S mall ceramic tube beads have been woven together on either side of a metallised plastic "Inca" disc. Then it is tied around the neck so that you can wear it as tight as you like. It will not take long to make, and you might find yourself wearing it every day. We have used black beads, but you could let your imagination run riot and even have a spectrum of colours around your neck.

YOU WILL NEED

For the necklace:
- 1 x 25 mm (1 in) metallized plastic Inca disc
- 16 Peruvian ceramic tubes
- 2 x 5 mm ($^1/_4$ in) black glass beads
- 60 x 4 mm ($^1/_6$ in) round black beads
- 12 x 3 mm ($^1/_8$ in) gold-plated balls
- 2 cards no. 5 black silk thread
- 13 ft (4 m) thick black thread

For the ear-rings:
- 2 x 18 mm ($^3/_4$ in) Inca discs
- 2 x 50 mm (2 in) gold-plated eyepins
- 4 x 3 mm ($^1/_8$ in) gold-plated balls
- 8 x 4 mm ($^1/_6$ in) black beads
- 1 pair gold-plated or gold earwires

Tools:
- **Round-nosed pliers for ear-rings**
- **Scissors**
- **Tape (optional)**

1 Unwind the silk on the cards, and knot the threads together about 18 cm (7 in) from the end. Thread on the first few beads and balls.

2 Thread into the first tube from either side, so that the threads cross inside it.

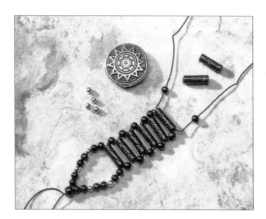

3 Add another 4 mm bead onto each of the threads before you thread into the next tube. Continue to weave in and out of the tubes until you have eight tubes on this side.

4 Thread the central beads and balls onto each thread and then bring both of them through the Inca disc.

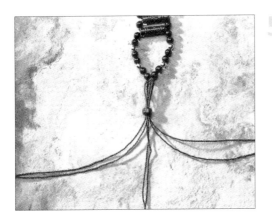

5 Repeat the weaving through the tubes on the other side of the Inca disc. Tighten the beads and tubes on the threads and then knot them together. Cut a 2 m (6 1/2 ft) length of thick black thread for each end, fold each in half, and attach them to the ends of the choker, by the knots. Slip a 5 mm (1/2 in) black bead on at each end, and braid the ends below these beads. Knot the end of the braiding and trim the ends. Thread the ear-rings onto the eyepins with a rolled top.

CERAMIC DISC BEAD AND CHAIN BELT

An idea for something different that you can make with beads. These large discs are from Rajastan and have lovely soft colours, but they are a little heavy for necklaces or ear-rings. So this is a design for a belt.

YOU WILL NEED

- 12 ceramic disc beads
- I packet 1.2 silver-plated wire
- 60 cm (2 ft) large link silver-coloured chain (from a **DIY** shop)
- 6 cm (2 ¹/₄ in) 0/8 silver-plated wire (optional)
- **Strong round-nosed pliers**
- **An extra pair of strong pliers**
- **Wirecutters**
- **File**

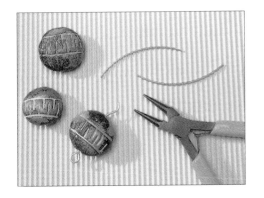

Cut lengths of wire to go through your discs (you will need about 6 cm (2 ¹/₂ in) for each bead). Make a large loop at each side of 11 of the beads. The 12th bead has one large and one small loop.

2 Open the chain in three-link lengths (you may need to use two pairs of pliers to do this), and link the chain and the beads together, ending with the 12th bead with the small loop at the very end.

3 Add two extra links of chain before the first bead. Make a hook with 6 cm (2 ¹/₂ in) of the thicker wire as shown in the techniques section. As an extra decoration you can wrap the thin wire around the hook, if you like.

TIFFANY STYLE NECKLACE

This pretty pastel and pearl necklace is threaded on to several strands of silk which are divided and brought back together again, creating a beautiful delicate effect. The large beads are pressed cotton balls that have been given an expensive-looking marbled finish by clever painting with nail varnish and watercolours.

YOU WILL NEED

- **Medium and large pressed cotton balls**
- **Knitting needle or wooden skewer**
- **Nail varnish in a variety of colours**
- **Watercolour paints**
- **Metallic felt pen**
- **Silk thread**
- **Beeswax cake**
- **Selection of small beads and bugles in differing sizes**
- **Fine needle**
- **Superglue**

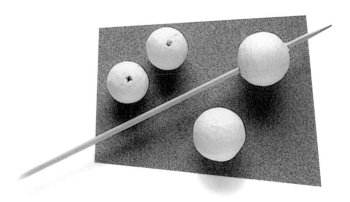

1 Pierce a hole through the centre of each cotton ball with a knitting needle or wooden skewer to form a bead.

2 Using a stippling motion, decorate the cotton ball beads with nail varnish and watercolour paints to create a marbled effect. Leave each coat to dry before applying the next. The watercolour paint sits on top of the nail varnish, adding to the effect. You may find it easier to paint the balls while they are on the needle or skewer.

3 *Complete the paint effect on the beads with lines drawn in metallic felt pen.*

4 *Decide on the length of the finished necklace, including the tassel. Cut the silk thread into four equal strands, each the required length. Draw the strands through the beeswax cake to coat them; this makes them stronger and easier to separate. Place them all together and fold in half to find the centre back. The necklace is worked from this point to the centre front, treating each side the same to create a symmetrical design.*

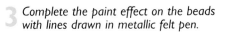

5 Thread all four strands through some small beads and bugles to sit along the centre back neck to start off the necklace. Next divide into two 2-strand sections. Work each of these identically, then bring back together by threading all four strands through one bead. Continue threading beads until you reach the centre front.

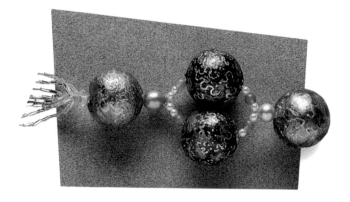

6 Take all eight threads (both sides) through two small beads then through a medium cotton ball bead, followed by a couple more smaller beads. Divide in half again and take each set of four strands through a few small beads, a cotton ball and a few more beads. Bring all eight back together through the final large cotton ball.

7 Each strand is now worked individually to create the tassel. Thread bugle beads on to each strand and finish with a small pearl. Wrap the strand back over the pearl, and using a needle, thread the strand back through the bugle beads. Knot each strand securely to itself at a convenient point and set the knot with a dab of glue.

PIPE-BEAD CHOKER

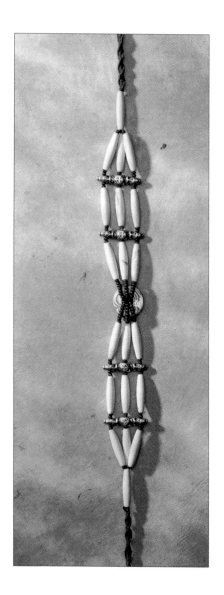

This is a nice easy way to use pipe beads and create a dramatic effect with them. The pipe beads are actually plastic but they look very natural. We have put them together with some elaborate spacer bars and a pretty ceramic ring to create a piece that is light and easy to wear.

YOU WILL NEED

- 1 ceramic ring
- 20 pipe beads
- 140 x 0/7 brown rocailles
- 4 spacer bars
- 360 cm (12 ft) waxed thread
- 280 cm (10 ½ ft) brown cord
- Scissors
- Glue
- Tape (optional)

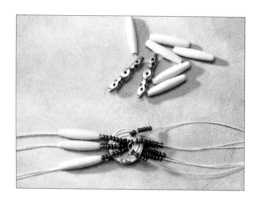

1 Cut 6 x 60 cm (2 ft) lengths of the waxed thread, and thread 16 rocailles onto each one. Thread three onto each side of the ceramic ring, and arrange the rocailles so that they are evenly positioned on the threads inside the ring.

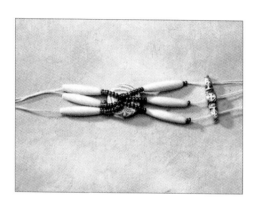

2 Now thread both ends of each thread through a pipe bead, so that you have three on each side, add the rocailles and work the double thread into a spacer bar.

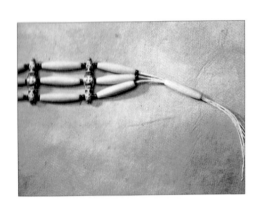

3 Work on into the second spacer bar and more pipe beads, and then work all the threads into a single pipe bead. Repeat on the other side of the ring. Move all the beads back up the threads so that there are no gaps.

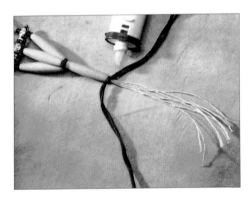

4 Cut two 140 cm (4 ft 7 in) lengths of the brown cord and tie one around each bunch of waxed threads. When you have tied the cords to the threads, add a drop of glue so that they will not slide down the waxed threads.

5 Braid each cord around the waxed threads, as shown in the techniques section. You may find it easier to tape the choker to your work top while you braid. Knot the ends of your braiding threads at the bottom of the waxed threads and leave trailing pieces of the brown cord.

CHARMS NECKLACE

This stylish necklace is made from a selection of small silvery beads with a matte, almost antique finish that conjures up an international look. The decorative metal charms are hollow, so they are lightweight, and can be easily obtained from your bead supplier. As an alternative, you can use genuine silver charms that look a little tarnished. Or try shiny, highly polished, silvery beads to produce more of a refined effect. If you have collected them, use bits and pieces from broken earrings and necklaces in a similar colour. Whatever charms you decide to wire, just make sure that they are similar in size. You won't need to make this necklace symmetrical (that is, position the same beads in the same place on both sides of the necklace) – just check that the overall design is visually balanced.

YOU WILL NEED

- **Tiger tail or nylon line**
- **2 crimp beads**
- **Small silvery beads**
- **11 to 15 hollow metal beads**
- **Same number of head pins**
- **Wire cutters**
- **Round-nosed pliers**
- **Needle-nosed pliers**
- **11 to 15 jump rings**
- **Small split ring**
- **Necklace clasp**

For this design, it isn't important to use exactly the same kind and number of beads on each side of the necklace. Just thread on similar sized beads, and place the charms at regular intervals, checking that the overall effect is balanced. Use tiger tail or nylon line that is approximately 61 cm (24 in) long.

Design Tips

- Before starting, sketch out your ideas on paper or lay the beads out on a flat surface to plan the design.

- Practice making perfect loops in the top of a head pin using round-nosed pliers. It is important that the loops close securely or the charms will fall off when the necklace is worn.

- If the holes of the charm are so big that the eye pins slip through them, add a small matching bead or rocaille to act as a stopper bead.

- Work the necklace backward from the centre to help with getting the balance right.

- Always select an odd number of charms – one for the centre and an even number for either side of the necklace.

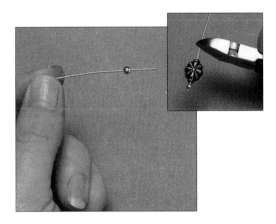

I Thread a small metal bead onto a head pin. Add a metal charm and trim the wire leaving approximately 1 cm (^{3}/$_8$ in).

2 Use round-nosed pliers to turn a loop in the top of the wire.

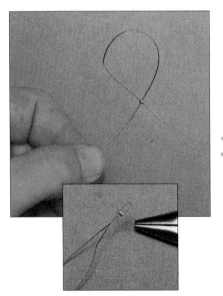

3 Cut the tiger tail to the required length. Thread on a crimp bead and push it close to one end. Make a loop and push the end of the tiger tail back through the crimp bead. Squeeze the crimp beads tightly with needle-nosed pliers to secure the loop.

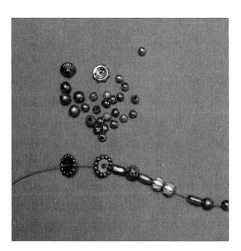

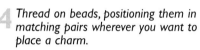

4 *Thread on beads, positioning them in matching pairs wherever you want to place a charm.*

5 *Slip a jump ring through the top of each charm and loop it over the tiger tail, between a pair of beads. Close to secure.*

6 *Thread on a crimp bead, make a loop in the tiger tail, and take the end back through the crimp. Squeeze tightly with pliers. Join a necklace clasp to the loop.*

RAINBOW COLLAR AND EARRINGS

I t was suggested that this could also
be called a Rasta necklace because of
the predominance of colours. This is a
very easy necklace to make, and it would
never go unnoticed.

YOU WILL NEED

- 17 x 36 mm (1 $\frac{1}{2}$ in) rainbow drops
- 14 x 20 mm ($\frac{3}{4}$ in) rainbow drops
- 26 x 5 mm ($\frac{1}{4}$ in) round beads
- 62 x 0/7 black rocailles
- 27 x 50 mm (2 in) eyepins
- 40 cm (1 ft 4 in) silk thread

Put your drop beads onto the eyepins,
clip of any extra length, and make loops
at the top of them. Four of the smaller
drops have rocailles, or round beads and
rocailles, above them.

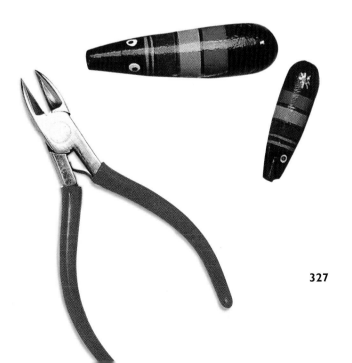

2 Make a knot at one end of the thread, and put a drop of glue onto the knot, then put a calotte over the knot. Thread your beads and the beads on eyepins onto the thread.

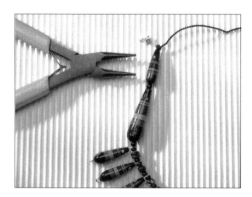

3 Again knot the silk at the end and put another calotte over the knot. Trim the loose ends of thread.

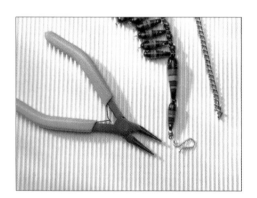

4 Add a piece of chain on one side of the necklace, and a hook to the other side, so that you can wear the collar at different lengths. The ear-rings are simply put onto the eyepins with rolled end.

COTTON BALL EARRINGS

YOU WILL NEED

- Large, medium and small pressed cotton balls
- Crafts knife
- Ear clips with integral loops
- Double epoxy glue
- Newspaper
- Wallpaper paste
- White acrylic paint
- Paint brush
- Wooden barbecue skewers
- Technical drawing pen (or nib and waterproof ink)
- Varnish
- Selection of small beads
- Eye and head pins
- Pliers
- Jump rings
- Strong thread
- Needle

These simple eye-catching earrings are made using the pressed cotton balls found in craft shops. They provide an ideal base for many pieces of jewellery and can be painted and decorated in a variety of ways.

329

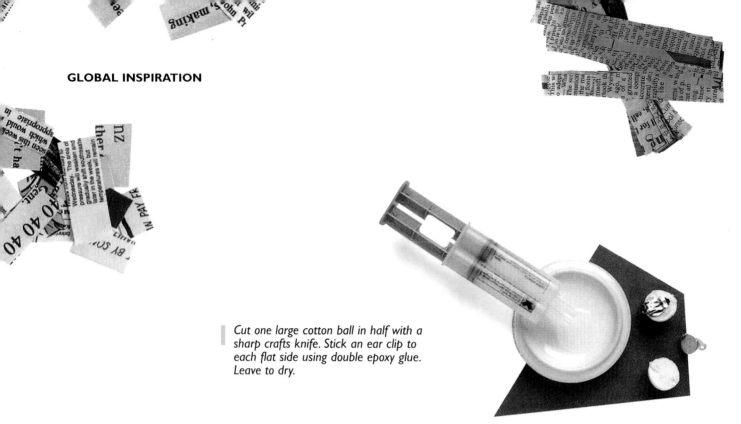

Cut one large cotton ball in half with a sharp crafts knife. Stick an ear clip to each flat side using double epoxy glue. Leave to dry.

2 Make up a quantity of wallpaper paste according to manufacturer's instructions. Tear up newspaper into small, neat strips and cover each cotton ball piece with three of four layers of pasted paper, making sure the back of each ear clip is well covered. The papier mâché ensures that the cutball has a smooth finish and the ear clip is secure.

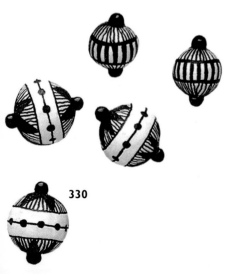

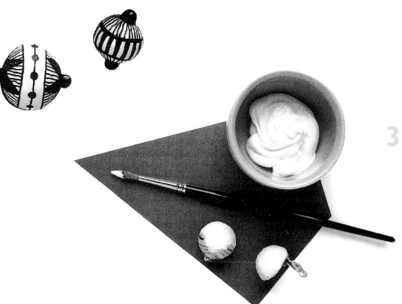

3 When the papier mâché is completely dry, paint with two coats of white acrylic paint.

4 Take the remaining cotton balls and pierce the centre of each one with barbecue skewers, gently twisting and pushing them through. Leave on the skewers and paint with two coats of acrylic paint. Stand in a suitable container or in plasticine to dry.

5 Leaving the beads on the skewers, draw on a pattern using a technical drawing pen or a nib and waterproof ink. If you prefer, you can draw the design first in soft pencil, then rub it off with an eraser once the ink is dry. Cover each bead with three or four coats of varnish and leave to dry.

6 To make up the earrings, thread a small bead then the bottom cotton-ball bead and another small bead on to a head pin. The small bead acts as a stopper and prevents the head pin ripping through the cotton bead. Thread the middle bead on to an eye pin in the same way. Using pliers, turn the top of the head pin and loop through the eye of the next bead to secure. Attach a jump ring through the loop of the ear clip, turn the end of the eye pin and join to the jump ring.

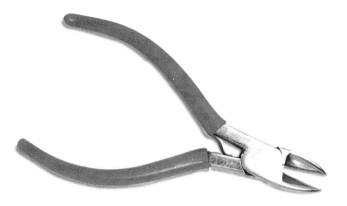

PERUVIAN NECKLACE

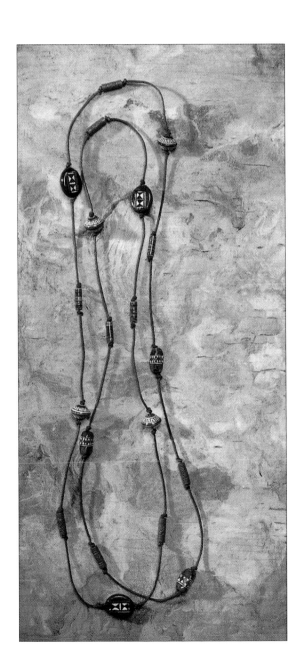

S imple but stylish – with a few tricks to make your necklace look really professional.

YOU WILL NEED

- **14 assorted glazed Peruvian beads**
- **5 plainer ceramic tubes**
- **Blue linen thread**
- **Measuring block**
- **Glue**
- **Needle**
- **Scissors**

333

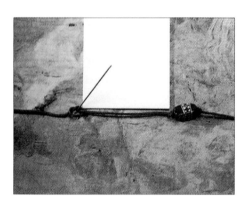

1 Cut a 180 cm (6 ft) length of the blue linen thread and position a bead in the middle of it. Make a knot either side of the bead and use a needle to move the knots close to the central bead. Use a measuring block to make the spaces between your beads. (Ours is 5 cm or roughly 2 in long). Position the block next to the knot that you have just made and use a needle to move another knot into position at the end of the block.

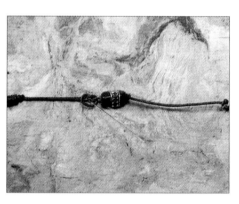

2 You can now thread another bead, and knot close to the other side of this bead. Continue with your beads, knots and spaces, working on both sides of the string, moving away from your central bead.

3 Thread both ends of the string through either side of your last bead.

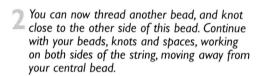

4 *Use your measuring block to check the distance between this bead and the ones on either side of it, and make a knot on both sides of the last bead. Put a drop of glue onto these knots and trim the ends of the string very neatly.*

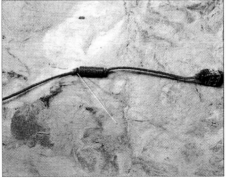

PERUVIAN NECKLACE

Variation on a Theme

This beautiful Peruvian necklace is made from lovely soft coloured beads, complemented by silver beads. It uses a variety of hand-carved Machu Picchu stone beads.

YOU WILL NEED

- 1 Machu Picchu stone "donut"
- 4 patterned ceramic beads
- 6 plain round ceramic beads
- 2 triangular Machu Picchu stone beads
- 2 square Machu Picchu stone beads
- 1 round Machu Picchu stone bead
- 1 long, flat Machu Picchu stone bead
- 10 brass discs
- 33 plain silver discs
- 2 granulated silver discs
- 2 round silver balls
- 2 x 7 mm (¼ in) jump rings
- 1 silver hook
- 4 French crimps
- Tiger Tail
- Jewellery wire
- 4 silver bead caps
- 3 silver round beads in two different designs

Cut a piece of wire, make a tiny loop at the bottom of it, put this through one of the silver faces, then roll the top of the wire. Wire around the donut wrapping round it several times and picking up the loop at the top of the face bead at the same time. Thread the beads onto a 70 cm (28 in) tiger tail, then crimp onto the jump rings at each end and finish with a silver hook.

INDIAN BRAIDED NECKLACE

T his is an effective way to use a few special beads, and makes an interesting change from putting them on leather. Use really bright threads that pick up the colours of the beads and make them look bright and beautiful.

YOU WILL NEED

- 10 assorted Indian metal beads
- 5 skeins of embroidery cotton in different colours
- Scissors
- Small piece of tiger tail
- Tape (optional)

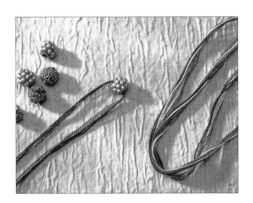

1 Cut 5 m (16 ¹/₂ ft) of each colour thread, which you will use double. Then cut two 1 m (3 ¹/₄ ft) lengths of two of the colours, which will go through the middle of the beads, as the core threads. Thread one of the beads onto the middle of these two pieces.

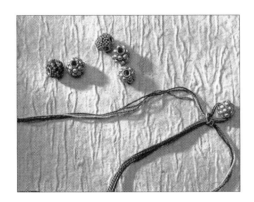

2 Knot the braiding threads onto the core threads. Start to braid over the core threads, as shown in the techniques section. You may find tape useful to hold the braid in place.

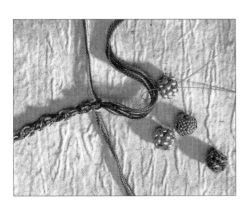

3 When you have made 11 cm (4 ¹/₂ in) of braiding, put a bead onto the corer threads. You may need to double the piece of tiger tail around the core threads to work them through the bead.

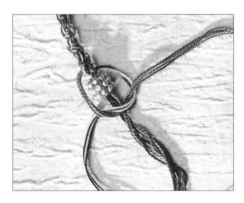

4 *Bring your braiding threads around the sides of the bead, and start to braid again on the other side.*

5 *Braid the threads 10 times between the beads. Continue to add the other eight beads.*

6 *When you have added all the beads, braid on for another 9 cm (3 1/2 in), and knot the threads together. Using the core threads and the braiding threads, make two tiny plaits, just long enough to go over a bead. Then knot all the threads together again, and trim the ends, so that they are all the same length.*

NATIVE AMERICAN BEADED BELT

A very bright cheerful representation of a Native American beaded belt. The one that we show here has patterns that we have designed, rather than authentic ones. If you wanted to make your belt more special, you could check original colours and designs in a library, and make yourself a more true representation.

YOU WILL NEED

- 50 g (2 oz) 0/7 yellow rocailles
- 10g (³/₈ oz) each of red, blue and green 0/7 rocailles
- Enough chamois leather to cut two pieces 4 x 48 cm (1 ¹/₂ x 19 in) + a small extra piece
- 8 x 8 mm (¹/₃ in) beads with wide holes (hair beads are good)
- Black polyester thread
- Beadloom
- Beading needles
- Needles
- Glue
- Scissors

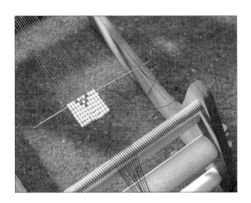

1 Thread your loom as shown in the techniques section, and start to work on your rocailles. There are 11 rocailles across the belt.

2 Follow the pattern, or design your own pattern and complete that. This beaded strip is 64 cm (2 ft 1 in) long. When you have taken it off the loom, work all the loose threads back into the work. Tie your warp threads together so that they can be hidden away.

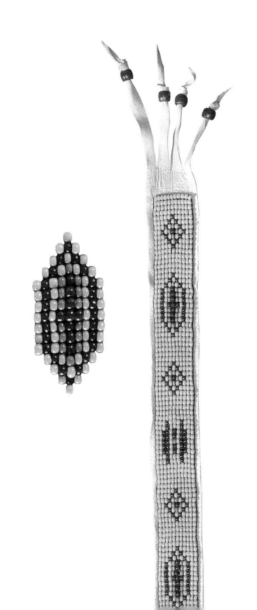

3 *Cut the two pieces of chamois. We have cut them from a piece from a motorist's shop. Sew the two strips together, and cut a small patch to go over the join.*

4 *Glue the beading to the chamois, making sure that the knotted warp threads are carefully tucked beneath the beading and the leather. Then sew the beading to the chamois for extra strength. Fringe the ends of the chamois.*

5 *Finally, thread on the beads and knot the fringes beneath the beads.*

As an authentic Indian touch, feathers could be added to the ends of the fringes. Add a loop of wire to the ends of the feathers and make little loops for hanging them.

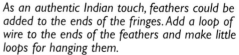

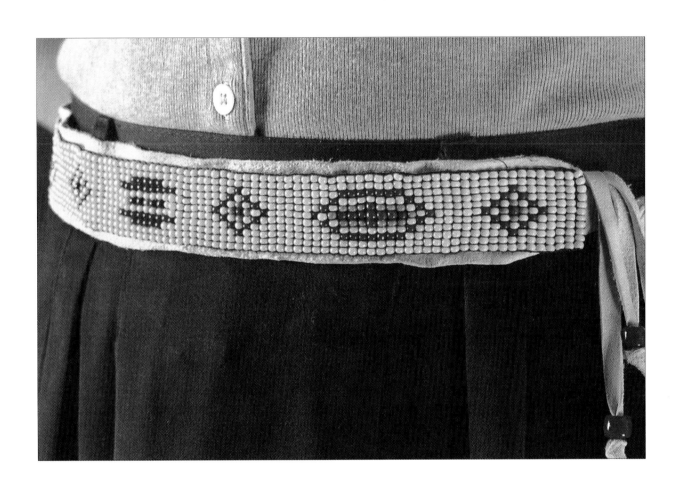

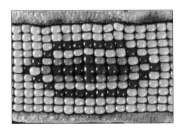

GLOBALLY INSPIRED
BEAD DECORATION

A plain, unpatterned piece of clothing or an item which looks a little tired can be jazzed up using some of the patterns, colours and materials we have just looked at.

     This is your chance to experiment and try out your design skills. Pick a souvenir from a holiday you have been on or perhaps something in a travel magazine that inspires you and get creative!

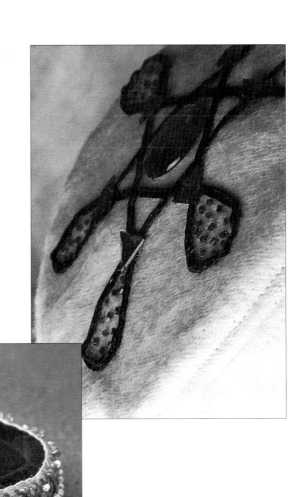

SPIDER'S WEB HAT

The hat was already interesting, but the design of it seemed to ask to have beads added and, of course, they ended up like spider's web. The strings of beads have been left loose on the hat, so that the movement becomes part of the design. The sample piece is shown flat for clarity and shows how you could add the stripes in beads too on a plain hat. We have not given precise amounts for the beads, as every hat (and head!) is different.

YOU WILL NEED

- **A hat**
- **Rocailles**
- **Bugles**
- **10 mm (¹/₂ in) round flat beads**
- **Small hearts**
- **Thread**
- **Needle**
- **Scissors**

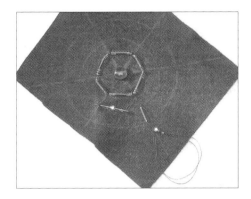 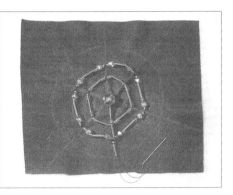

1 & 2 *The sections of beads are strung onto the thread and then a small stitch is made to attach that section to the hat. If your hat has a lining, open a small section, so that you can work from both sides. You can then restitch it later.*

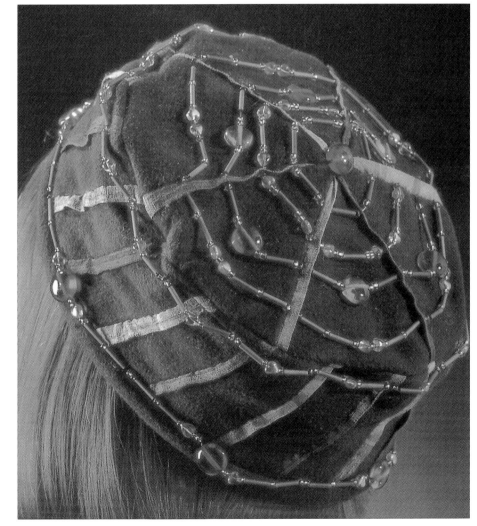

EMBROIDERED HAT

Variation on a Theme

Use your braid and beads on this pill-box hat to match your clothes and make yourself the centre of attention. The same method could be used to decorate a beret.

To attach the trim, first find the central point of the top of the hat and use the pen to mark it. Draw two equilateral triangles, with sides about 6.5 cm (2¹/₂ in) long, so that the corners form a six-pointed star and the centre of the star is at the centre of the hat. Extend the corners of the triangles to form loops.

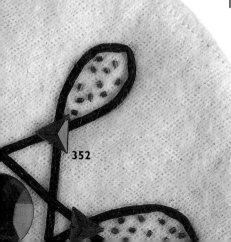

Next, starting at one corner, pin the braid along the lines of one of the triangles and around the loops. Sew the braid in place. Repeat with the other triangle and loops.

YOU WILL NEED
• **6 flat, triangular, red beads**
• **3 gm (¹/₈ oz) red, two-cut, silver-line rocaille beads, size 12/0**
• **1 large, round, flat, red bead**
• **Beading thread**
• **1 plain pill-box hat**
• **Water-erasable marking pen**
• **Ruler**
• **2.5 m (approximately 8 ft) black braid**
• **Dressmaking pins**
• **Sewing needle**

Use the marking pen to make a regular zigzag pattern around the edge of the hat. On our hat, each line was about 40 mm (1 ¹/₂ in) long. Pin, then stitch the braid in place.

To add the beads, sew a red triangular bead to each point of the star. Sew individual rocailles in a random pattern in the middle of each of the loops, taking the thread through to the inside of the hat after attaching each bead. Sew the large round bead in the middle of the star.

BEADED HAIR BRAID

With a piece of braid, a selection of beads in several shades of the same colour, and a little imagination, you can transform a basic fabric band into a striking hair decoration. Braids available for dressmaking and home furnishing can be used for the ideas shown here. They can be plain, or patterned in smooth or textured finishes, and come in every colour imaginable. For this project, a colourful braid was carefully beaded in coordinating colours to highlight the bold pattern and sewn with invisible thread to a plain padded band. The sparkling sequinned variation was bought already beaded and is perfect for special evenings. A silky textured braid wrapped around a plain band and finished with ribbon roses could be worn by a bridesmaid for a summer wedding.

YOU WILL NEED

- **Padded fabric hair band**
- **Tape measure**
- **Length of braid (about 45 cm/18 in, depending on the band)**
- **All-purpose, clear-drying glue**
- **Selection of coordinating embroidery beads**
- **Beading needle**
- **Thread in several shades of the same colour**
- **Invisible thread**
- **Scissors**

To determine the amount of beads you will use when decorating your own braid, count the number of beads used in one inch of braid and multiply by the length of the band.

1   *Measure the band and add 2.5 cm (1 in) to allow for two 1.3 cm (½ in) hems.*

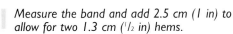

2   *Cut the braid to the correct length.*

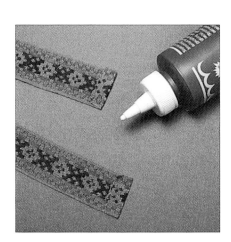

3   *Turn 1.3 cm (½ in) to the wrong side at each end and glue in place or hem with invisible thread.*

Design Tips

- You don't need a long length of braid; interesting bargain buys can be found in end-of-roll boxes.

- Look for ornate braids, especially beaded ones, at antique fairs to make a really special band.

- Experiment and plan your design before working on the real thing – use double-sided tape to secure in position temporarily.

- Plain bands can be bought from jewellery suppliers and painted with acrylic paints to coordinate with your chosen braid.

- As an alternative to braids, embroider plain fabric covered bands with colourful threads. To add further texture and shape to the band, work the design using simple stitches threaded with beads or sequins.

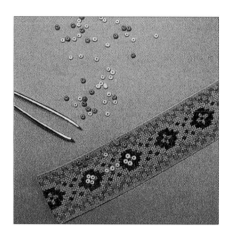

4 Using the braid's pattern as a guide, work out where you are going to stitch the beads. For this design, beads in the two main colours of the braid were used to highlight the geometric pattern.

5 Sew one colour in place first, working clusters on the same length of thread and single beads individually. Use a tiny backstitch under each bead to hold them in position securely.

6 Sew the second coloured beads in place in the same way as the first.

7 Oversew the braid to the band using invisible thread, taking care to keep the tension even.

HAIR ACCESSORIES
Variation on a Theme

Beads look wonderfully effective when used to trim almost any kind of hair accessory, whether to coordinate the accessory with a special outfit or simply to transform daywear to evening wear.

With just a little imagination and an assortment of beads you can produce the most original hair accessories. Choose beads to go with the base materials and, depending on whether this is "soft" or "hard", sew or glue the beads in place. Wrap the ribbon around the accessories and glue in place before sewing on the beads.

Try decorating tortoiseshell Alice bands, slides and hair combs with creamy pearl beads or small rocailles. Fabric scrunchies can be edged with small beads and plastic canvas cut into barrette shapes and decorated with ornate bead work.

Experiment and plan your designs before securing the beads in place. This is not always easy on narrow, curved surfaces, so used double-sided adhesive tape to hold the beads temporarily. If you are sewing the beads, you may find a fine, curved needle useful for awkward angles. Choose a matching or invisible thread or add some extra texture to the design by sewing on the beads with fine ribbon or raffia.

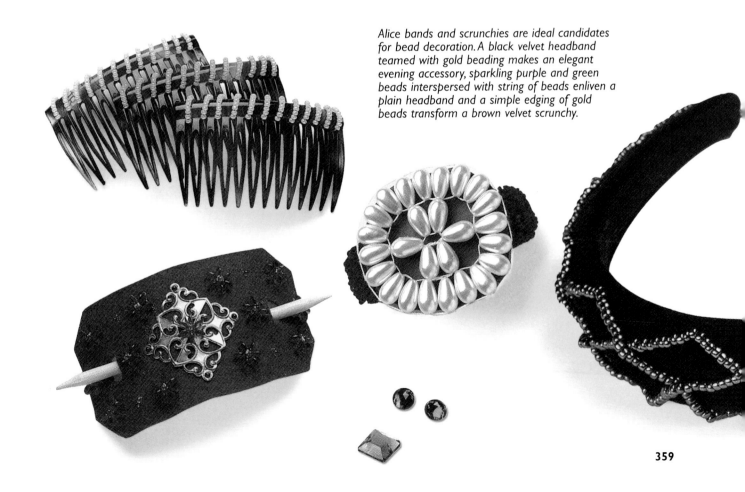

Alice bands and scrunchies are ideal candidates for bead decoration. A black velvet headband teamed with gold beading makes an elegant evening accessory, sparkling purple and green beads interspersed with string of beads enliven a plain headband and a simple edging of gold beads transform a brown velvet scrunchy.

359

HISTORICAL STYLE

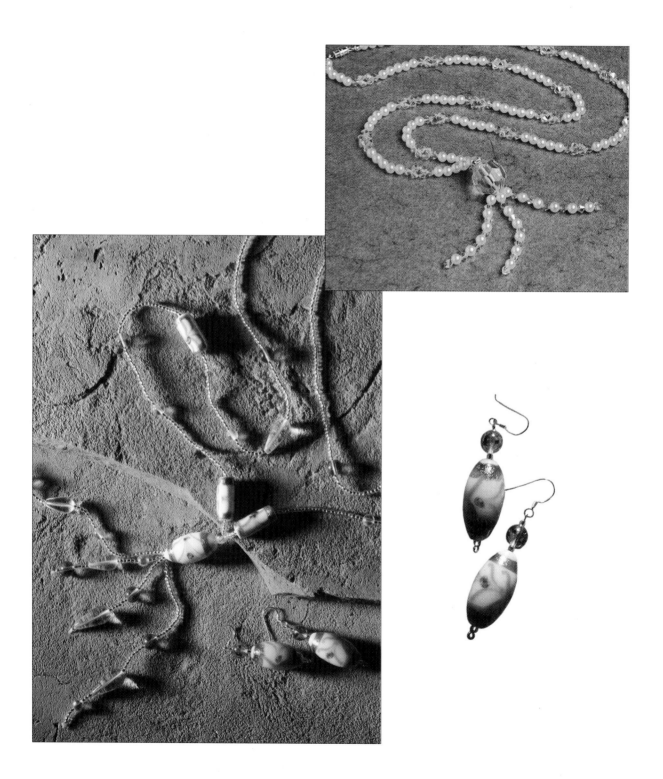

The designs in this section are taken from bygone eras. The 1920's Art Deco era for example is a great inspiration for jewellery design.

Look at antiques books and recreate the styles that still look classic and chic today.

ART DECO BEADWORK

Weaving beads on a loom is a traditional craft, used for centuries to make all kinds of jewellery. This bracelet is worked in pearly-white, black and silver-grey, in a simple design that is evocative of the 1920s. It is a perfect introduction to the basic techniques and will inspire you to create your own designs. The earrings are worked in the same colours to coordinate but are woven by hand rather than on the loom.

YOU WILL NEED

- **Beadweaving loom**
- **Pearly-white, black and silver-grey beads**
- **Tape measure**
- **Fine strong white thread**
- **Fine beading needle**

1 Measure your wrist loosely with a tape measure. If the weaving area of your loom is longer than this, measure the loom from end to end, between the places where the thread is fastened. Add 12.5 cm (5 in) to your wrist or loom measurement (whichever is bigger) then double this and cut six threads to this length. Fold them in half and knot the loose ends together so that you have a loop of threads at one end.

2 Put the loops over one of the pegs on the loom and the knot over the other end. Turn the bar until the threads are almost taut, then separate the threads and spread them out over the dividers. (Don't worry if the threads are further apart than your beads are wide, as you can tighten as you go.) Tighten the fitting to make the threads as taut as possible. These are the warp threads.

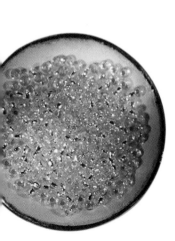

3 Take a long thread in your beading needle and thread on 11 white beads. Place the thread with the beads on to the warp threads about 2.5 cm (1 in) from the looped end and tuck each bead into the spaces between the threads. Leaving a long end for weaving in later, push down the beads so that they jut out underneath the warp threads and then bring the needle back through the beads, keeping them under the warp. Hold the end of the thread so that it doesn't come straight through, and pull the row tight.

4 Working from the chart, pick up the beads as shown for each row and add them to the warp thread in the same way as for Step 3. When nearing the end of a thread, leave a long tail after finishing a row and start another thread by running the needle through the last few rows. If you reach the end of the loom before you have worked the required length, turn the bar at the end to move the weaving on. Continue weaving until your bracelet is about 2.5 cm (1 in) shorter than your wrist measurement.

5 To make the "eye", pick up nine beads and lay them centrally on the warp threads. Bring the needle back through the beads as before, passing the needle through the gap instead of around the end. Pick up seven beads for the next row and work as before. Work three rows of two beads at one side of the seven, then repeat the other side to match.

6 Take seven beads on to the thread and lay them over the top of the rows of two beads. Take the needle through the first two beads underneath the warp threads, then take it over the warp for the next three so that it is not caught in, going back under for the last two beads. Repeat this row, then join these last two rows together by sewing into the first bead on one row, then the second on the other, the third bead on the first row, etc. Weave the thread back through a few rows to fasten off.

7 To make the bar of the fastening, go back to the start of the weaving and pick up nine beads as in Step 5. Pick up seven beads for the next row and five for the following row and work as before. Add three rows of three beads, then thread on 15 beads and take the needle back through the last row to make a loop of beads. Flatten the loop so that you have two rows of nine beads, including the three beads of the last row. Join these two rows together by stitching into the first bead on one row followed by the second on the other, the third on the first row, etc. Finish by weaving the thread back through a few rows to fasten off.

8 Take the remaining ends of threads back through a few rows and cut close to the weaving. Remove the bracelet from the loom and thread all the ends of the warp threads back into the bracelet in the same manner.

Other examples of loomwork

Left: Evening bag
Right: Beaded choker

TIFFANY STYLE NECKLACE AND EARRINGS

P ale and delicate with lovely porcelain beads and shimmering glass. The necklace is made to wear long, with an exciting cluster of beads at waist length. There are simple earrings to compliment it.

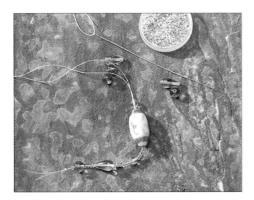

Cut 2.5 m (8 ft) of thread and use it double with a needle. Knot the ends and put glue onto the knot. When the glue is dry, thread the first beads and drops and rocailles onto the thread and then the large oval bead.

YOU WILL NEED

For the necklace:
- 1 oval porcelain bead
- 4 tube shape porcelain beads
- 8 x $^1/_3$ in (8 mm) pink glass beads
- 8 x $^1/_4$ in (6 mm) clear glass beads
- 4 large clear glass drops
- 2 small clear glass drops
- 20 g ($^3/_4$ oz) 0/9 clear rocailles
- 3 m (10 ft) white polyester thread

For the ear-rings:
- 2 oval porcelain beads
- 6 clear rocailles
- 2 x $^1/_3$ in (8 mm) pink beads
- 2 x 50 mm (2 in) eyepins
- 1 pair earwires

Tools:
- Scissors
- Needle
- Glue
- Round-nosed pliers for the ear-rings

2 Thread on, working the round beads, tubes and drops into the rocailles and making a long plain area for the back of the necklace. Keep working back down the necklace, whilst checking that the two sides are matching. Now thread back into the round bead, rocaille and oval porcelain bead near the beginning of the necklace. Put on the last few beads and knot at the end. Put a drop of glue onto the knot.

3 Cut another 50 cm (1ft 8 in) length of thread, and use it double with a needle again. Knot and glue the end and thread a few more of the hanging beads. Carefully knot this thread under the oval bead and above the hanging pieces.

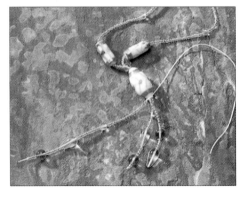

4 Thread on the last few beads and knot the end of this thread. Trim off the loose ends.

5 The earrings are simply made by putting the beads onto the eyepins with a rolled top.

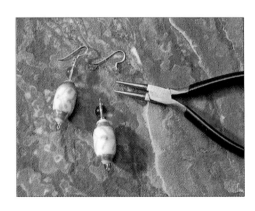

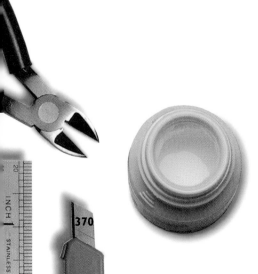

1930'S STYLE PEARL AND GLASS BEADS NECKLACE

The decades of the 1920s and 1930s, the era of the flapper and of art deco design, produced truly creative jewellery design that is still very popular today. Style books on this period can be excellent sources of inspiration for your own individual designs. This 1930s-inspired necklace is worked in a sophisticated combination of pearls and rosettes of crystal beads and finished with a central, elegant, beaded tassel that was all the rage at the time. The touch of sparkle from the light-reflecting crystals gives this particular bead combination the magic and formality perfect for evening wear. To transform this necklace for a more relaxed look, choose different colours, styles, and even bead sizes.

YOU WILL NEED

- **2 calotte crimps**
- **Pliers**
- **Strong cotton thread**
- **Small pearls and crystal beads**
- **2 fine needles**
- **1 diamanté rondelle**
- **1 large crystal bead**
- **Glue (optional)**
- **Necklace clasp**

Cut 4 strands of thread to the length required for each side of the necklace (including the tassel) plus 31 cm/12 in. Knot the strands together in pairs and thread each pair through a calotte. With the knot sitting neatly in the cup of the calotte, use a pair of pliers to secure it firmly over the threads.

Each side of this necklace comprises 2 pieces of thread, 112 cm (44 in) long the thread pair is divided, beaded individually, and then bought back together again to create the crystal rosettes. When each side is the length you want, take the threads of both through a large central bead and then bead each individual thread to form the tassel. Use an odd number of beaded strands for the tassels.

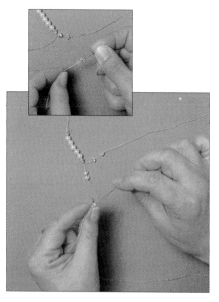

2 Working one side at a time, thread each length of cotton thread through a needle and then take both needles through 5 pearls and 1 crystal. Separate the threads and add 2 crystals to each. Bring the threads together again by taking both needles through a crystal. Pull the threads taut and push the beads back toward the calotte, making sure the crystals form an even shape.

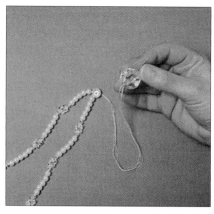

3 Repeat steps 2 and 3 until each side is the right length to begin working the tassel, making sure both sides are identical. Take all four strands through the diamanté rondelle and then through the large crystal bead.

Design Tips

- *Use vintage beads to produce an antique finish, especially for designs inspired by the past.*
- *To make a larger tassel with more beaded strands, work each side of the necklace on three or four threads instead of two. Remember that tassels always look better with an odd number of strands.*
- *Experiment by adding more beads to each single strand of thread. If you opt for more than two threads on each side, try beading all of them before bringing them back together through a single bead.*
- *Twisting or braiding the divided strands can create spectacular effects.*
- *Use the same basic techniques to create different effects with alternative bead styles. Try substituting bugle beads for the pearls, and glass rocailles for the crystals to give the necklace a more delicate finish.*

4 Work 2 of the 4 threads together. Thread each with alternating pearl and crystal beads to the length required. Wrap the thread around the last bead, and take the needle back through the rest of the beads on the strand and the large crystal.

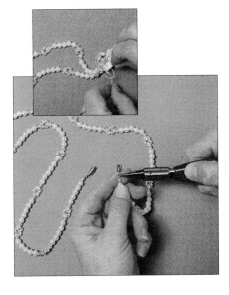

5 When all the strands have been worked, knot the threads securely together between the crystal and the rondelle. Add a dab of glue to secure the knot if required. To finish, slip the loop on the necklace clasp and secure using pliers.

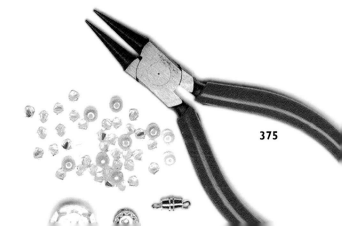

375

As a variation on this necklace, why not try using wooden beads in contrasting colours, which is a less formal look than the diamonds.

A decorative filigree cap and hanger have been added to the 3 strand necklace below to complete the shimmering effect.

Other examples of pearl and glass combinations

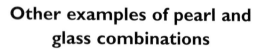

FLOWERS, LEAVES AND BEADS

This is a delicate, pretty necklace with pastel leaves and flowers, which is very light and easy to wear in the summer.

YOU WILL NEED

- 8 tiny plastic flowers
- 8 larger flowers
- 8 smaller leaves
- 5 larger leaves
- 4 white glass drop beads
- 13 figure 8 findings
- 16 x 2.5 cm (1 in) silver-plated headpins
- 38 x 6 mm (¼ in) clear beads
- 76 x 0/7 pearl rocailles
- 16 x 0/7 clear rocailles
- 30 x 6 mm (¼ in) clear glass beads
- 8 x 8 mm (⅓ in) pink glass beads
- Tiger tail
- 4 french crimps
- Fastener
- Round-nosed pliers
- Necklace pliers
- Scissors

1 | Put the leaves onto the figure 8 findings.

2 Put the headpins into the flowers (with a rocaille inside them) and make a loop on top of them.

3 Arrange your flowers, leaves and beads onto the tiger tail and crimp the fastener on at either end.

4 The finished necklace.

By using a colourful version of the leaf bead, the necklace will have a totally different, modern feel.

Top: The plain hairslide has been jazzed up by simply gluing a few silk flowers to the top.

Middle: This badge style pin is just one of the many designs you could copy from natural objects. It is made out of rubber.

Bottom: These ear-rings are inspired by nature too. They are made simply from an ear hook and a jump ring attached to a hand made Fimo leaf.

HISTORICAL STYLE
BEAD DECORATION

Historical jewellery, costumes and even buildings use intricate patterns to add detail and interest. These can be used as inspiration for jewellery. Rich colour and fabrics give a luxurious feel.

EMBROIDERED HAIR FASTENER

The use of fabric in jewellery design has added another dimension to the craft and opened up a whole new world of design ideas. If you can use a needle and thread, you can transform remnants of fabric, scraps of embroidery thread, and leftover beads into pretty barrettes. Simple embroidery stitches worked by hand or on the sewing machine add texture and detail to simple fabric shapes – choose several subtle shades of the same colour for a dainty finish or bold, bright metallics for something more flamboyant. Complementary beads and sequins can be used as delicate highlights or in greater numbers to create a rich, ornate finished look.

YOU WILL NEED

- **Cardboard**
- **Compass**
- **Pencil**
- **Scissors**
- **Felt (12.5 cm/5 in square)**
- **Piece of firm iron-on interfacing**
- **Embroidery silk**
- **Embroidery needle**
- **Sequins**
- **Tiny embroidery pearl beads**
- **Single-hole punch**
- **Plastic needle to fasten the barrette**
- **Iron-on adhesive**

Transforming your finished design into a barrette is easy with the wide range of iron-on adhesives available they fuse the fabric to cardboard, leather and even wood.

To draw an oval, first draw a circle 5 cm (2 in) in diameter. With the compass set to the same measurement, move the point to the edge of the circle and draw an arc, taking the pencil from edge to edge, passing across the centre point of the drawn circle.

1 Draw an oval on the cardboard and cut it out. Place the interfacing on the felt and cut to size, then iron on following the instructions provided.

2 Place the cardboard template on top of the interfacing, trace it in pencil, and cut it out.

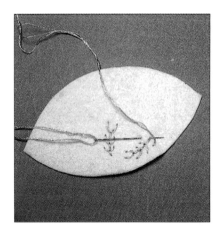

3 Mark the position of your chosen motifs on the interfacing. Using two strands of silk, embroider the design – this design is worked in a pretty feather stitch.

4 Add sequins as required. Working with a single strand of silk, bring the needle through the central hole of the sequin from the wrong side. Take the needle through a tiny pearl bead and back through the central hole of the sequin. Tie off on the wrong side.

Design Tips

- *Sketch out your design on paper first and work out the position of the embroidered motifs and any bead detail.*

- *Look for manuals on embroidery stitches and experiment with different styles on spare scraps of fabric.*

- *Study patterned fabrics for suitable motifs to make barrette shapes and highlight the design with beads and embroidery stitches.*

- *If your piece of fabric is large enough, you will find it easier to work on if it is held taut in an embroidery hoop.*

- *Textured fabric paints with metallic or glitter finishes are a great way to jazz up a simple piece of material.*

- *Ironing the wrong side of the fabric to a firm interfacing makes drawing shapes and cutting them out easier.*

5 Measure and mark the positions for the barrette-pin holes and cut out using a hole punch. The holes should be placed in line with the points of the oval and approximately 1.9 cm ($^3/_4$ in) in from the edges, depending on the size of the fastening pin.

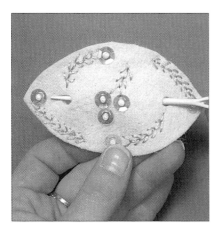

6 Check the length of the fastening pin and set the holes appropriately so it sits centrally on the motif as shown.

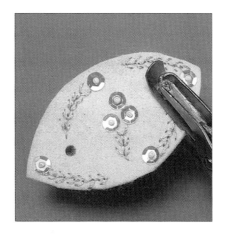

7 Cut another oval from the remaining felt and apply iron-on adhesive to one side following the instructions. Remove the paper backing and place the embroidered motif right-side down on top of a towel. Place the adhesive side of the second oval on top, matching edges exactly and press following the instructions provided.

SHOE PATCHES
Variation on a Theme

The quantities given here are sufficient to make one pair of beaded shoe patches. Use half the quantity and the same technique to make a decoration for a handbag or a garment.

Iron a piece of interfacing to the wrong side of one square of fabric. Draw a circle with a diameter of about 5 cm (2 in) on a piece of pattern paper and cut it out. Place this on the fabric and draw around the outline with a chalk pencil. Do not cut out the circle yet.

Find the centre of the circle and bring the thread through to the front. Pick up a turquoise sequin and a silver bead. Take the thread back through the sequin so that the bead holds it in place.

YOU WILL NEED

- **Beads and thread**
- **2 turquoise sequins**
- **10 gm (¹/₂ oz) silver rocaille beads, size 12/0**
- **110 gm (¹/₂ oz) turquoise rocaille beads, size 12/0**
- **120 turquoise bugles**
- **60 silver bugles**
- **Beading thread**
- **1 pair of shoe clips**
- **Medium-weight, iron-on, black interfacing, 4 pieces each 10 x 10 cm (4 x 4 in)**
- **Medium-weight black fabric, 2 pieces each 10 x 10 cm (4 x 4 in)**
- **Pattern paper**
- **Scissors**
- **Beading needle**
- **Dressmaker's chalk pencil**
- **Contact adhesive (optional)**

Bring the needle through to the front, close to the edge of the sequin, and pick up two turquoise rocailles. Lay them flat on the fabric, curving them around the sequin, and take the needle to the wrong side of the fabric. Bring it back through to the front between the rocailles and take the thread through the second rocaille. Pick up two more rocailles and continue in this way until you have completed the circle.

Make a circle of 12/0 silver rocailles next. Bring the needle through to the front of the fabric and pick up four beads. Lay these against the turquoise rocailles and take the needle through to the back. Bring it to the front between the second and third silver beads and take the thread through the third and fourth beads before picking up four more beads. Continue in this way until you have completed the circle. Continue to work circles of alternating turquoise and silver rocailles until you have four complete circles of each.

In the next circle, pick up four silver rocailles, securing them as before, then four turquoise rocailles. Repeat the groups of four, alternating the colours around the circle. On the next row, alternate groups of four silver rocailles with five

turquoise rocailles. Work two complete circles with silver. The final row of silver should be approximately on the chalk circle.

Bring your needle through to the right side as close to the circle of silver beads as possible and pick up a turquoise bugle. This should be positioned at 90 degrees to the silver bead and the base of the bugle should touch the silver bead. Take your needle through to the wrong side to hold the bugle in position and bring it back through to the right side, as close as possible to the next silver bead. Pick up another turquoise bugle and stitch it in place so that there is a tiny gap between the bugles at the outside edge. Continue to add bugles all around the circle. We used alternating groups of six turquoise and three silver bugles.

Cover up the stitches on the back of the finished pieces by carefully ironing on a second piece of interfacing. Using very sharp scissors, trim away the excess fabric and interfacing to within 2 mm ($^{1}/_{8}$ in) of the bugles. Stitch or glue a shoe clip to the back of each circle.

389

7.3

MODERN STYLE

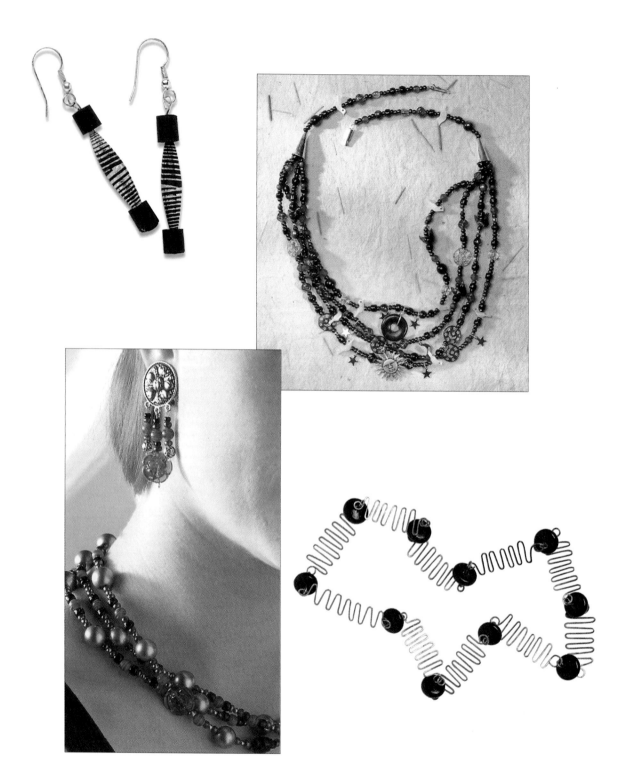

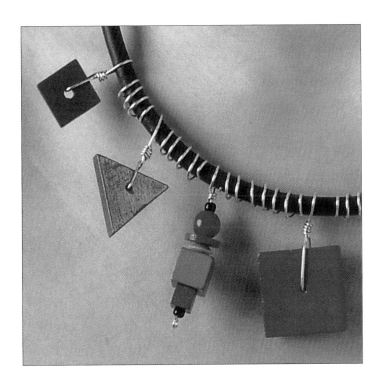

These projects are so much fun and so is the final product!

Bold colours and shapes make these designs really eyecatching – they will be great conversation starters.

WIRE AND BEAD NECKLACE

This simple yet bold neckpiece uses contrasting brass wire and black beads to create a rhythmic folded wire necklace.

YOU WILL NEED

- Ruler
- Wire snips
- 360 cm (4 yards) of 1.1 mm (14 gauge) brass wire
- Round-nosed pliers
- Protective gloves
- 10 flat round glass beads
- 2 pairs flat-nosed pliers

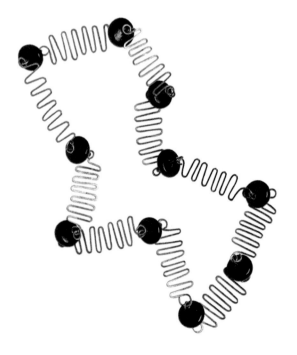

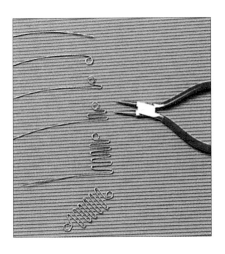

1 With the wire snips, cut ten 30cm (12 in) lengths of brass wire. Make loops on the ends of each length of wire, using a pair of round-nosed pliers. Then, take the pliers and bend the wire back and forth on itself to produce an undulating pattern approximately 2.5 cm (1 in) wide. Repeat the process until nearly all of the wire has been used up. Finish by making another connecting loop with the round-nosed pliers.

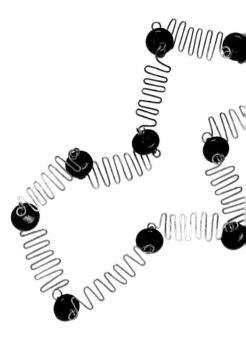

2 Using a hammer, tap the wires gently on a firm surface so that they become flattened. Wear protective gloves.

3 Using wire snips, cut ten 2.5cm (1 in) lengths of brass wire. Using the round-nosed pliers, make a loop at on end of the wire. Gently tap the looped wires on a firm surface to flatten them.

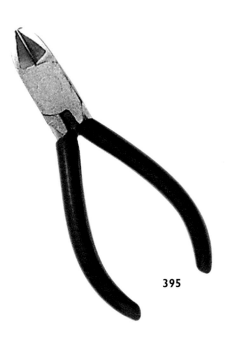

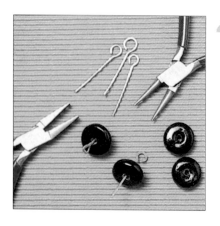

4 Thread a glass bead onto each short wire and with a pair of round-nosed pliers, make a loop at the other end of the wire to secure the bead.

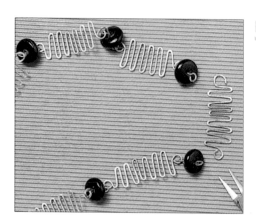

5 Using two pairs of flat-nosed pliers, open up the loops of all the sections and connect the loops together, in the sequence shown, for form the necklace.

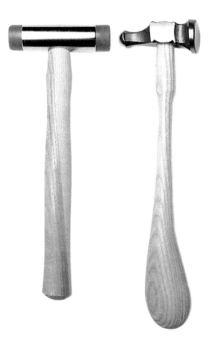

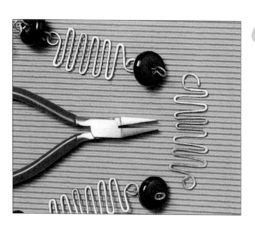

6 Close the loops with the flat-nosed pliers, making sure that all of the linked loops are securely fastened together.

MODERN ART CHOKER AND EARRINGS

Not all projects with beads need to have lots of threading. With this necklace we have wired most of the beads so that they hang flat, and threaded a few, to create a bright, primary choker.

YOU WILL NEED

For the choker:
- 1 wooden square bead
- 1 blue circle bead
- 1 pink triangle bead
- 1 mauve small square bead
- 2 small blue cubes
- 2 green cubes
- 2 yellow lice beads
- 2 red washer beads
- 2 pink round beads
- 4x 0/7 black rocailles
- 1 round black tubing
- 1 packet of 0.8 jewellery wire
- 4cm (1½ ft) 1.2 jewellery wire

For the ear-rings:
- 2 Mauve small square beads
- 2 Pink triangle beads
- 2 Red washer beads
- 2 Yellow lice beads
- 2 Large green cubes
- 2 Small blue cubes
- 2 Pink round beads
- 8 x 0/7 black rocailles
- 2 x 50 mm (2 in) eyepins
- 2 x 25 mm (1 in) eyepins
- 1 pair earwires

Tools:
- **Round-nosed pliers**
- **Wirecutters**
- **Flat-nosed pliers**

1 Start by wiring the beads that are going to hang flat, as shown in the techniques section. Check that the loop you make is large enough for the rubber tubing to go through, before you make the coils at the bottom of it. Cut about 8 cm (3 in) of wire for each bead.

2 Cut another two pieces of wire the same length, make a neat loop at the bottom, and thread on the beads, to make the hanging pieces. Make a large loop above the beads so that it will go over the rubber tubing and coil your wire below it.

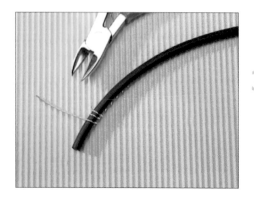

3 Use the end of the rubber tubing to make the spirals that go round it.

4 Thread the design onto the tubing and gently press the ends of the spirals into the rubber so that the pattern remains separated. You can gently press in the loops above the beads as well, so that they stay in place.

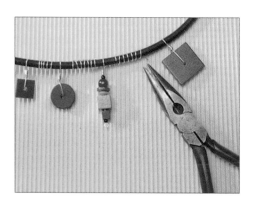

Some more examples of jewellery inspired by modern art.

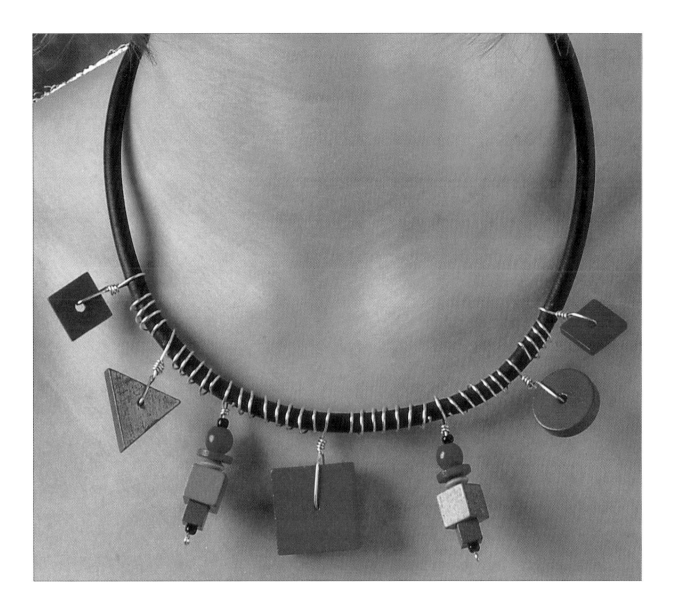

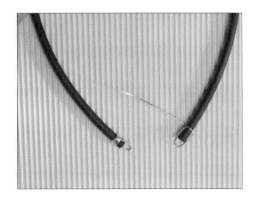

5 Make another loop at the end of the rubber tubing, turn the wire at an angle to it, and wind the wire round the loose end. Attach a hook to this and hook it into the other side to fasten the choker. Make the ear-rings by linking the two eyepins together when you have threaded the beads.

WOODEN NECKLACE AND BRACELET

Variation on a Theme

This colourful set is great fun to make. The techniques are quite simple, the emphasis being on the variety of colours and shapes. The beads are made by a German toy manufacturer, so it seems a good idea to get the children to help make the jewellery.

Necklace

Cut the thread to the required length and thread the beads as shown or to you own design.

At the end of both sides knot the thread on to the hook and jump ring. Thread the loose end of the thread on a needle and work it back down the beads.

YOU WILL NEED

- **25 cm (10 in) 1.2 mm (¹/₂ in) sliver plated wire**
- **24 small flat washer beads**
- **16 large flat washed beads**
- **3 green cubes**
- **2 small blue cubes**
- **2 flat square beads**
- **Round-nosed pliers**
- **Necklace pliers**
- **Wire cutters**
- **File**
- **Needle**
- **Scissors**

You could make these fun earrings and complete the set.

Bracelet

Cut 20 cm (8 in) of wire, file on end and roll it into a loop. Thread on your beads.

Clip off any excess wire, leaving enough to match your first rolled end, file the end of the wire and roll in into a loop. Attach your own hook to one of the loops.

WIRE AND GLASS BEAD BROOCH

O ne continuous length of silver wire is decorated with beads and twisted to create an abstract form.

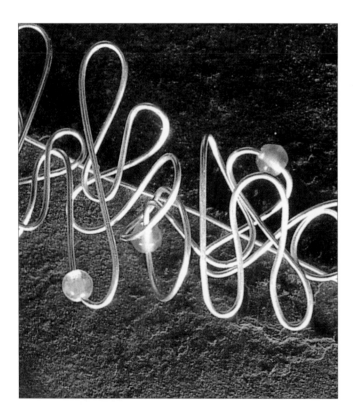

YOU WILL NEED

- **90 cm (36 in) of 1.1 mm (14 gauge) silver wire**
- **Round-nosed pliers**
- **8 beads with 1 mm ($^1/_{25}$ in) hole**
- **Wire cutters**
- **Needle file**
- **Nylon mallet**

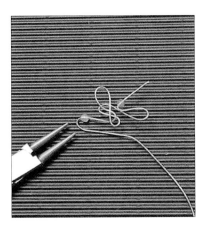

1 Leaving a 2 cm (³/₄ in) straight piece of wire at the start, begin to curl and bend the remainder of the silver wire into an interesting form.

2 Thread the beads as you go to give an even spread throughout the design.

3 Having produced the final design, curl back the remaining wire to form the pin and cut to the right length. Use the 2 cm (³/₄ in) of wire at the opposite side of the brooch to make a safety hook.

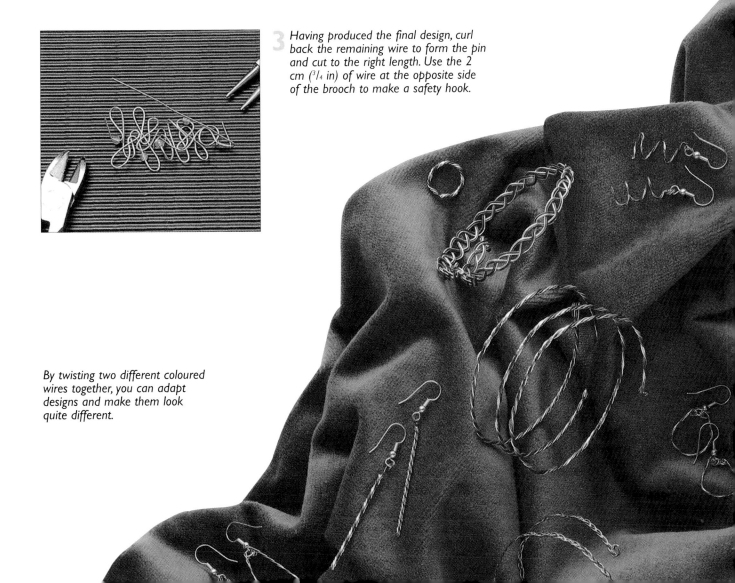

By twisting two different coloured wires together, you can adapt designs and make them look quite different.

4 *File a fine point for the pin, then gently hammer the pin with the nylon mallet.*

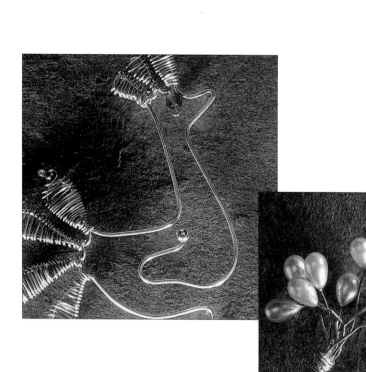

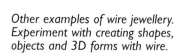

Other examples of wire jewellery. Experiment with creating shapes, objects and 3D forms with wire.

RUBBER AND BEADS NECKLACE

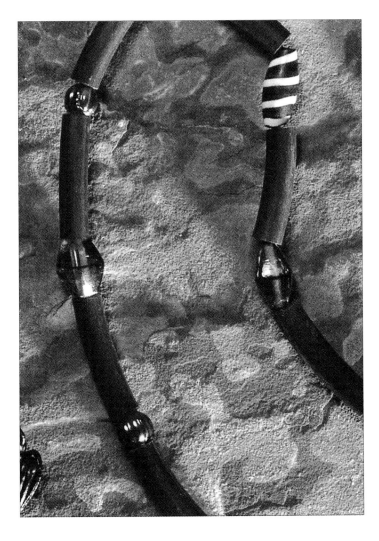

E xtruded rubber tube is used in striking contrast with large, bright beads to create a highly tactile and modern necklace.

YOU WILL NEED

- **Craft knife**
- **60 cm (24 in) of 0.8 mm (11 gauge) black rubber tube**
- **76 cm (30 in) of black leather thong**
- **Scissors**
- **14 varied glass beads**

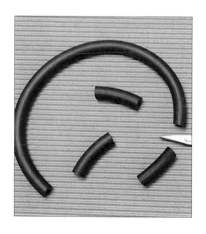

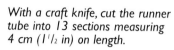

1 With a craft knife, cut the runner tube into 13 sections measuring 4 cm (1¹/₂ in) on length.

2 Tie a knot in one end of the thong. Thread the rubber tubes and beads onto the leather thong. Thread the rubber tubes and beads onto the leather thong in the order shown.

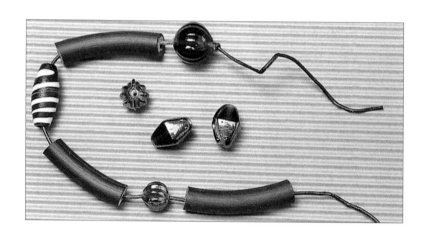

3 When all of the components are threaded, tie a know in the other end of the leather thong and trim the ends using scissors.

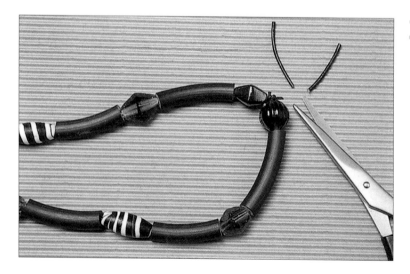

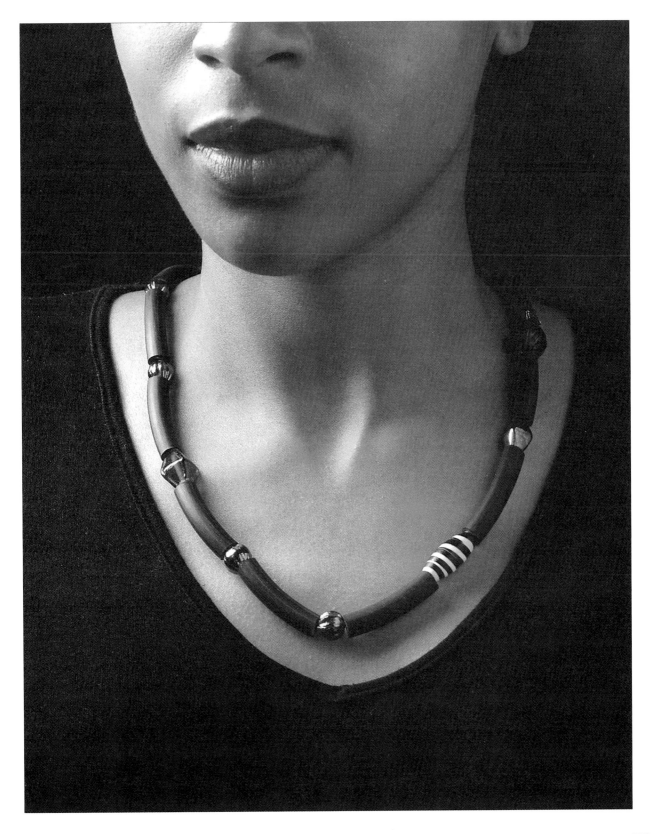

ROLLED PAPER BEAD NECKLACE AND EARRINGS

B eads are available in a wide variety of materials. The ones here resemble fine china, but they are made from tightly rolled up strips of wrapping paper and are as light as a feather. They look exquisite strung together, and nobody would guess they are just paper!

YOU WILL NEED

- **Sheets of wrapping paper – 1 or 2 patterned, 2 black, 1 silver**
- **Gold quilling paper (for tiny beads)**
- **Pencil**
- **Metal ruler**
- **Crafts knife or scissors**
- **Quilling tool or fine knitting needle**
- **PVA glue**
- **Needle**
- **Strong thread**
- **Head pins**
- **Pliers**
- **Ear wires**
- **Spray varnish (optional)**

410

1 Using a pencil, mark the long edge of a sheet of patterned paper on the wrong side with the widths of beads required – we used 11 x 2 cm (³/₄ in), 13 x 12 mm (¹/₂ in) and 13 x 2.5 cm (1 in). Mark the same widths on the opposite edge then draw parallel lines between the marks. Cut out the strips using a craft knife and metal ruler or scissors. Cut all but two of the strips in half (leave two 12 mm (¹/₂ in) strips uncut to make the earrings). Take six strips of gold quilling paper and cut each into eight equal lengths.

2 Using a quilling tool, or your fingers and a fine knitting needle, roll up a strip of paper tightly to make a cylinder-shaped bead, leaving a big enough hole in the centre to fit the thread through. Stick down the end of the paper with as little glue as possible and hold the bead for a moment while the glue sets. Roll up the rest of the strips, gluing as before, then roll up the quilling paper to make tiny gold beads.

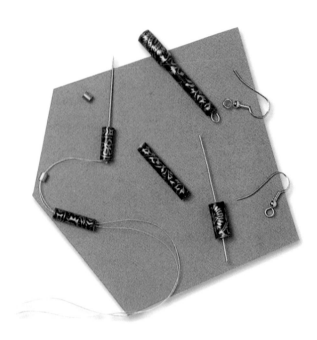

3 Make up an earring by threading one fat 12 mm (¹/₂ in) bead and one 2.5 cm (1 in) bead on to a head pin. Use pliers to turn a loop at the top of the pin and then attach an ear wire to this. Make the other earring in the same way. Thread the remaining beads on to strong thread to make a necklace, using them in the following order – 2.5 (1 in), 12 mm (¹/₂ in), 2 cm (³/₄ in), 12 mm (¹/₂ in). Repeat to the end, threading tiny gold beads between each paper bead. Spray with varnish, if required, to make them last longer.

4 To make the black and silver oval beads cut a 30 cm (12 in) square of wrapping paper in each colour. On the wrong side of each square mark one edge at 2.5 cm (1 in) intervals, then mark its opposite edge 12 mm (¹/₂ in) in and then at 2.5 cm (1 in) intervals. Draw in lines between the marks and cut out the elongated triangles, discarding the two at the edge as they will not be the correct shape. Cut 30 cm x 15 cm (12 in x 6 in) rectangle of black paper into straight 6 mm x 30 cm (¹/₄ in x 12 in) strips.

5 Lay a silver triangle over a black one so that a narrow edge of black can be seen. Starting from the wide end, roll the two strips together as before and glue the ends in place. Roll the straight black strips up tightly to form small beads to use between the ovals. Make the beads up into earrings and necklace.

6 Different types of paper create exciting effects when rolled up to form beads. Try recycling birthday and Christmas wrapping papers or even old magazines. Creases can be ironed out using a low heat setting, and if you don't like the final effect you can always paint the beads with nail varnish or enamel.

'DONUTS' NECKLACE AND EARRINGS

These ceramic beads from Greece come in soft, mottled colours. You could just wire one of the "donuts" and wear it on a thong, or you can make something really extrovert like the necklace shown here.

YOU WILL NEED

For the necklace:
- **8 ceramic donuts**
- **2 spacer beads**
- **27 grey cube beads**
- **42 blue round beads**
- **4 long grey beads**
- **56 x 4 mm ($^1/_6$ in) purple beads**
- **2 cones**
- **180 cm (6ft) thread**
- **1 packet 0.8 wire**

For the ear-rings:
- **2 donuts**
- **2 blue round beads**
- **2 grey cube beads**
- **6 x 4 mm ($^1/_6$ in) purple beads**
- **0.8 wire**
- **2 x 38 mm (1 $^1/_2$ in) eyepins**
- **1 pair earwires**

Tools:
- **Round-nosed pliers**
- **Necklace pliers**
- **Scissors**

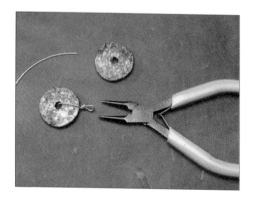

Wire the "donuts", as shown in the techniques section. Then cut three 60 cm (2 ft) lengths of thread and plan the beads and donuts onto the threads, so that they hang well together.

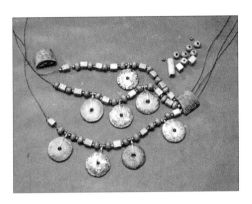

2 *Take your threads through the spacer beads when you are happy with the design.*

3 *Bring all your threads through the beads on the side pieces.*

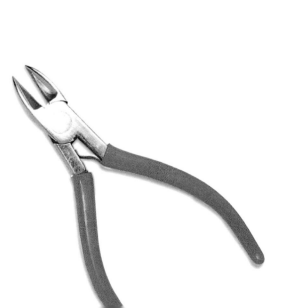

4 Crimp the end of each of the threads, making a small loop. Then cut a short piece of wire, make a loop on its end and hook the ends of the threads into this loop. Put the cones over the wire and turn another loop to attach the fastener.

5 The ear-rings are made by wiring the "donuts" and attaching an eyepin to the wire for the top beads.

Other examples of 'donut' necklaces

BEADED METAL STICK PIN

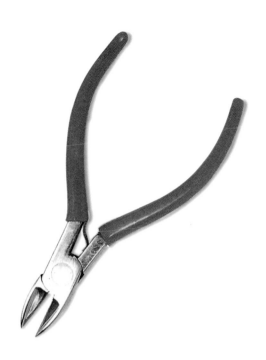

Together with beads, jeweller's wire rates as one of the most essential and versatile materials to have in your craft jewellery box. It comes in a variety of thicknesses and colours – red, gold, silver and copper, plus plated alternatives that are less expensive. The wire can be used to make your own basic findings or for more decorative work like these contemporary pins. The metal is soft enough to be shaped into intricate designs using a variety of objects as basic forms, from pliers to pieces of wood. The finished piece can then be attached to a purchased stick pin or to one made from the same metal and filed to a point at one end. Decorated with jewels or beads, the finished pins can be designed to coordinate with a favourite hat or outfit.

YOU WILL NEED

- **Jeweller's Wire**
- **Wire cutters**
- **Needle-nosed pliers**
- **Several beads with large centre holes**
- **All-purpose, clear-drying glue**
- **Stick pin with protective cap**

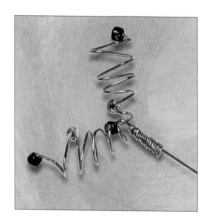

This piece requires jeweller's wire about 1.2 mm ($\frac{1}{21}$ in) thick for the metal swirls and 0.8 mm ($\frac{1}{31}$ in) thick for binding the metal swirls to the stick pin.

Design Tips

- *Choose a pin to suit the use of the design – lapel pins are shorter than hat pins.*
- *Experiment by bending jeweller's wire around different shapes to create a variety of designs.*
- *The wire can also be hammered into shape to create a completely different effect – use thicker wires and a rawhide hammer or an ordinary hammer covered with a piece of suede or felt.*
- *Look for unusual feathers – perhaps from an unused feather duster.*
- *Beads with large holes can be slipped on after the wire has been shaped and glued to secure, or you can try beading the wire first and then carefully shaping it for a more ornate finish.*

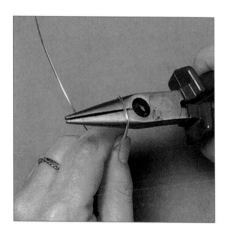

1 Cut 2 pieces of thick wire, each 25.5 cm /10 in long, and grip one end with the widest end of the pliers.

2 Wrap the wire around the pliers 5 or 6 times, working toward the tip. Trim the wire, leaving a short tail, and slip the coil off the pliers. Repeat for the other piece.

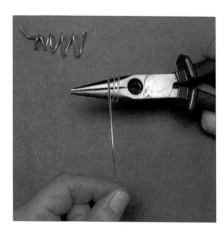

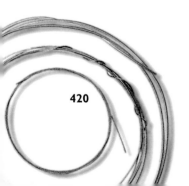

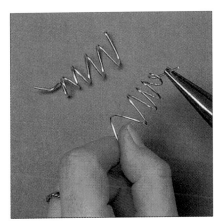

3 Holding the widest end of the coil with your fingers and the other end with the pliers, gently stretch out the coil. Straighten the tail at the narrowest point with pliers.

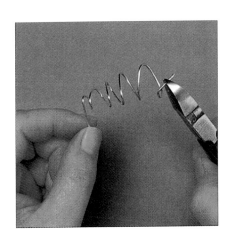

4 Trim the end of the first wrap to approximately ¼ cm/ ½ in.

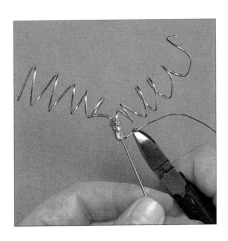

5 Place the top of the stick pin between the 2 tails left at the narrower ends of the coils and bind them together tightly with fine wire. Wrap the wire evenly and trim when the joint feels totally secure.

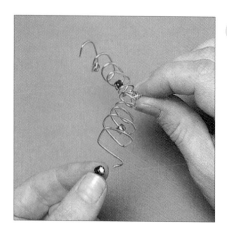

6 *Straighten out the tips at the other end enough to slip on the beads. Add as many beads as you want, slipping them over the coils toward the centre but leaving them spaced out. Fold the tips of the wire back on themselves to form hooks and glue the beads securely.*

7 *The beads in the centre can be glued or left loose for an interesting effect.*

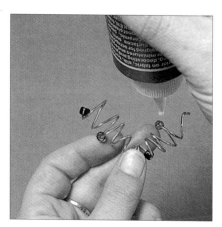

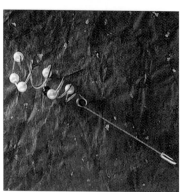

Other examples of stick pins

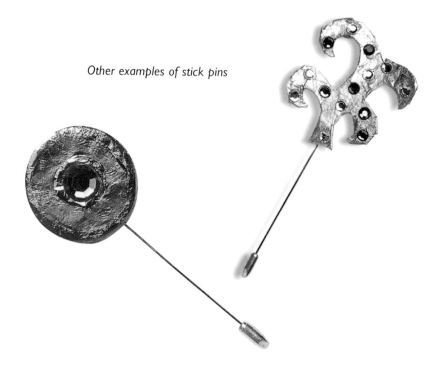

EARRINGS, NECKLACE AND BRACELET

This set is a lovely mixture of bright colours and dull silver-coloured beads. We started our design with the clips for the earrings and added the glass rose beads to compliment the fruit and flowers pattern on them. Next came the smart bracelet, again with little roses, and finally a simple twist necklace with the last few glass roses entwined in it.

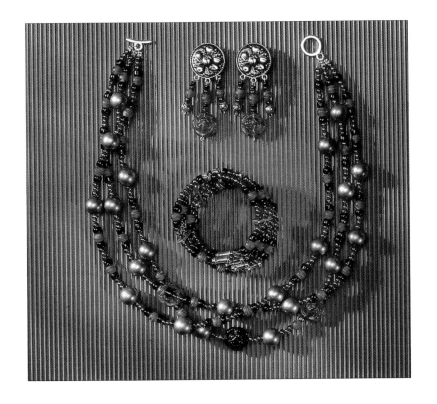

YOU WILL NEED

For the necklace:
- 21 x 5 cm (2 in) metallized plastic balls
- 35 x 6 mm (¹/₄ in) frosted lamp beads
- 64 x 5 mm (¹/₅ in) black glass beads
- 132 x 0/6 red rocailles
- 58 x 3 mm (¹/₈ in) turquoise balls
- 3 glass roses
- 12 french crimps
- 1 bar, and circle fastener
- Tiger tail or thread

For the bracelet:
- 80 x 0/6 red rocailles
- 48 x 3 mm (¹/₈ in) turquoise balls
- 4 x metallized plastic roses
- 40 x 5 mm (¹/₅ in) black glass beads
- 16 x frosted lamp beads
- 2 x 2-hole spacer bars
- 2 x 3-hole spacer bars
- 4 circles of sprung bracelet wire
- 8 safety ends

For the ear-rings:
- 2 ornate clips
- 6 x 50 mm (2 in) eyepins
- 8 x 0/7 black rocailles
- 6 x frosted lamp beads
- 2 glass roses
- 12 x 0/6 red rocailles
- 5 x metallized plastic roses

Tools:
- **Necklace pliers**
- **Round-nosed pliers**
- **Scissors**
- **Wirecutters**
- **Glue**

I For the necklace cut three 45 cm (1 ¹/₂ ft) lengths of tiger tail and attach them to one end of the fastener with crimps. Thread the beads and crimp again at the other end. The necklace can be worn plain or twisted.

2 To make the ear-rings, thread the beads onto the eyepins, clip them to length, and roll the tops to attach them to the clips.

3 Now thread beads onto the top two wires and add a three-hole spacer to these new wires. Join in the top wire from the first pair. Work on round on all of the wire, putting the same pattern into the centre.

4 The bracelet is the most complicated piece to make. Cut the lengths of wire and glue four safety ends to each of them. Thread the first few beads onto the bottom two wires and thread on a two-hole spacer bar.

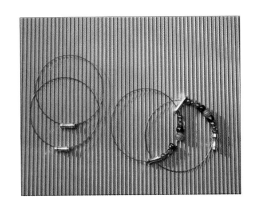

425

5 Reverse the pattern round to the other side adding the other spacer bars. Then glue the safety ends to the other side to keep all the beads in place.

NIGHT-SKY NECKLACE

YOU WILL NEED

- 1 haematite donut 20 mm ($^3/_4$ in)
- 1 sun
- 6 round mosque beads
- 12 cube mosque beads
- 10 mother-of-pearl birds
- 84 x 5 or 6 mm ($^1/_4$ in) glass beads in black, purple, and blues
- 2 tiny heart beads
- 6 black ceramic birds
- 15 iridescent miracle beads (6 - 8 mm/$^1/_4$ - $^1/_3$ in)
- 6 stars
- 2 moons
- A few 3 mm ($^1/_8$ in) silver-plated balls
- 350 x 0/7 dark iridescent rocailles
- 2 cones
- Fastener
- Tiger tail
- French crimps
- 0/8 silver wire
- 9 figure-8 fittings
- Black polyester thread
- Necklace pliers
- Wirecutters
- Scissors
- Round-nosed pliers

Multi-strands of stars, moons and birds and a dramatic haematite donut, all hanging from tiny dark iridescent rocailles.

1 Cut a 6 cm (2 ³/₄ in) piece of wire, put it through the donut and cross the ends over. Form one end into a neat loop with your pliers. Use your fingers to wrap the other wire around the bottom of this loop. When you have covered the bottom of the loop with a few neat coils, clip off any extra wire and press the end of the wire into the loop above the coils with your pliers. The figure-8 fittings are used to hang the sun, and the tiny stars and moons.

2 Cut four 50 cm (1 ft 8 in) lengths of thread and start to thread on your beads. The donut and the sun should be in the same position on the threads. Space all the bigger beads and the hanging pieces in the more central part of the strands, and work towards plainer, smaller beads at the sides. You need to keep a selection of beads to go either side of the cones. When you feel that your threading is right, hold the strands up to see how they hang. If you want them all to hang together, the strand with the donut should be the shortest.

3 Finish all of the ends by making neat loops with the french crimps, then trim any loose ends. Cut a 12 cm (5 in) length of tiger tail for each end and make a loop at one end with crimps. Thread the tiger tail through the ends of the necklace strands and back into its own loop. Thread a cone over the ends of the necklace strands.

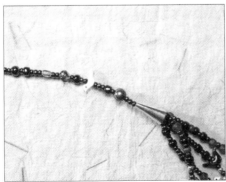

4 Your last few beads are then threaded onto the tiger tail, and you can attach the fastener at the ends with more french crimps. Finally trim any loose ends.

MODERN STYLE
BEAD DECORATION

It is so easy to make beautiful gifts or household decorations out of plain items.

You can add extra sparkle to seasonal decorations which no one else will have – they are so simple you could even get the children involved!

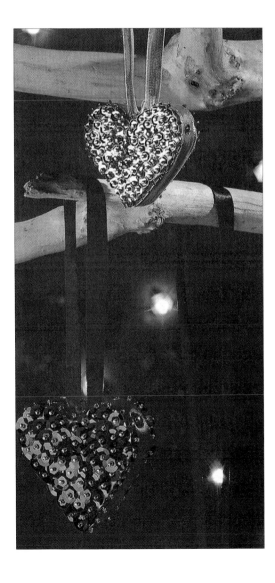

DECORATIVE FRAME

This is an easy way to make more of a plain frame. The colours of the beads gave the idea for the bunch of grapes design but the scope is enormous and you could really let yourself go with ideas for decoration.

YOU WILL NEED

- I frame
- 100 x 4 mm ($^1/_6$ in) purple beads
- 100 x 0/7 grey rocailles
- 40 x 0/8 green rocailles
- 15 x turquoise bugles
- Fine black polyester
- Thread
- Strong glue
- Needle (to move beads)

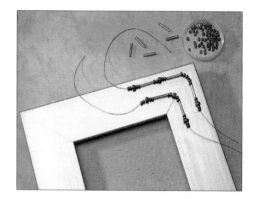

1 You could either make your design on paper first, or just arrange the beads onto the frame and then move them off a piece at a time to add the glue.

2 The bugles are best threaded onto short pieces of thread to glue them into place. When the glue is dry, you can remove the pieces of thread.

FRAME

Variation on a Theme

Y ou can paint a plain wooden frame with silver before you begin. Spray paint or model-maker's silver paint work well but leave the paint to dry before you start to glue.

Place the frame on the sheet of paper and use a pencil to trace the outlines of the inner and outer edges.

Using the outline as a template, experiment with the arrangement of the largest flat, mirrored beads. Position the smaller mirrored beads among the larger beads and move them around until you are happy with the design.

Lay the frame next to the template and, keeping to the pattern you have chosen, begin to glue the large beads in place. Once all the flat beads are in place, leave to dry for at least an hour.

Add the bugle beads one by one, working on small sections of the frame at a time. Apply a smear of glue to the frame and use a beading

needle to help position the beads, which should be placed in various directions to create interesting textural effects.

Add the rocailles two or three at a time, with the help of a beading needle, until all the gaps have been filled. Leave to dry overnight.

YOU WILL NEED

- 3 flat, round 30 mm (1 $^1/_5$ in) silver beads
- 1 flat, round 25 mm (1 in) blue bead
- 1 flat, round 25 mm (1 in) amethyst bead
- 2 flat, round 12 mm ($^1/_2$ in) amethyst bead
- 5 flat, round 12 mm ($^1/_2$ in) silver bead
- 19 flat, square silver bead
- 3 flat, square blue beads
- 5 flat, square amethyst beads
- 12 flat, triangular silver beads.
- 2 flat, diamond shaped turquoise beads
- 8 flat, oval shaped blue beads
- 1 oz (25 gm) 8 mm ($^1/_3$ in) silver bugle beads
- 1 oz (25 gm) 12 mm ($^1/_2$ in) silver bugle beads
- 1 oz (25 gm) 5 mm ($^1/_5$ in) blue bugle beads
- 1 packet transparent rocaille beads
- 1 packet blue rocaille beads
- 1 packet turquoise rocaille beads
- 1 picture frame, 9 $^1/_2$ x 8 in (24 x 20 cm) with sides 4 cm (1 $^1/_2$ in) wide
- 1 sheet plain, white paper, slightly larger than frame
- Pencil
- Clear, all-purpose glue
- Beading needle

CHRISTMAS BALLS

Variation on a Theme – Gluing

YOU WILL NEED

- **Beads**
- **5 gm (0.25 oz) silver rocaille beads, size 12/0**
- **2 gm (0.125 oz) 5 mm ($^{1}/_{5}$ in) purple sequins**
- **2 gm (0.125 oz) 8 mm ($^{1}/_{3}$ in) purple sequins**
- **2 gm (0.125 oz) 5 mm ($^{1}/_{5}$ in) silver sequins**
- **1 m (3 ft) purple ribbon, 7 mm ($^{3}/_{8}$ in) wide**
- **Clear nail varnish**
- **Scissors**
- **Short dressmaking pins**
- **Ruler or tape measure**
- **Polystyrene ball, 6 cm (2 $^{1}/_{2}$ in) in diameter**
- **Thimble**

Most craft shops and the haberdashery departments of large stores stock polystyrene balls. Be sure to use a thimble to protect your pinning finger when making these decorations.

Attaching the Ribbon

Cut a piece of ribbon about 20 cm (8 in) long. Pick up a silver rocaille and small purple sequin on a pin and stick the pin through the centre of the ribbon.

Take the remaining ribbon and measure 20 cm (8 in) from one end. Pass the pin used in step 1 through this point so that the two lengths of ribbon are at right angles to each other.

Stick the pin into the ball and bring the

ribbons around the sides so that the surface of the ball is divided into four equal sections.

Bring the two short ends together at the opposite side of the ball and hold with a pin. Assemble the other ends at the same point and pin, leaving the long end loose.

Dab nail varnish on the cut end of the ribbon to prevent fraying. When dry, make a loop with the long end. Pick up a rocaille and small sequin on a pin. Use the pin to hold the three short ends and the end of the loop in place.

Decorating the Ball

Pick up a rocaille and a large purple sequin on a pin and place them in the middle of one of the segments.

Surround the purple sequin with eight rocailles and silver sequins and pin two small purple sequins and rocailles at the top of the circle of silver sequins. Repeat on the bottom of the circle. Pin a row of silver sequins and rocailles next to the ribbon and all around the edge of the segment.

Fill in the remaining space with large purple sequins, keeping the rows as straight as you can. Repeat until the other three sections are filled.

GLOSSARY

Acrylic: A plastic resin used by some contemporary jewellers since the 1960's. It can be moulded and cut, has a wide colour range and is sometimes used in conjunction with metals.

Anneal: To soften metal by heating and cooling at the correct temperature. Soft metal is easier to work.

Anvil: Heavy metal stand with flat top and a bottom with a round protruding nose. Used for shaping, flattening, hardening, etc.

Argotec: A white powder mixed to a paste with either denatured alcohol or water and then painted onto silver prior to heating to avoid fire stain.

Arkansas Stone: An abrasive stone used for sharpening graving tools and fine points. Should be kept well oiled in use.

Barrel Polisher: Rubber barrel containing small stainless steel burnishers which polishes small chains and rounded pieces by a continuous revolving movement.

Bearer Wire: The metal ring inside the bezel which forms the "shelf" on which the stone sits.

Bevel: The slope on the edge of a metal surface.

Bezel: The part of a ring which encompasses and fastens the stone.

Binding Wire: Steel wire which ties and holds parts together for soldering.

Borax: A flux used for soldering. It is mixed to a paste with water and painted onto the areas to be soldered.

Burnisher: Highly polished hand-held stainless steel tool. Used to produce a shiny surface by rubbing on metal.

Cabochon: A polished precious or semiprecious stone which is rounded, not cut into facets.

Casting: A means of making an object by pouring molten metal into a shaped space, usually by burning out a wax model of the object.

Cat's Eye: A general terms for several varieties of gemstone which, in certain lights when cut, exhibits a luminous moving line.

This is most notable in the lustrous yellowish-brown variety of Chrysoberyl.

Charcoal Block: Used in soldering as a level surface. Can be scraped and shaped as necessary, and reflects heat well.

Chasing: Pushing or punching a line onto the front of metal to form a design or a series of lines.

Chenier: Silver/gold tubing. Can have walls of different thickness for different uses, such as hinges, choker, and joints.

Claw Setting: A setting for a faceted stone which uses wires or "claws" to hold the stone. It has an open back which allows the light to reflect off the stone.

Coping Saw: A hand saw used like a jeweller's saw for cutting wood, plastics, etc.

Cotter Pin: Used for holding pieces together while soldering. If passed through a hole, the two ends can be bent over to keep the tension.

Culet: The bottom edge of a faceted stone.

Dividers: Metal implement with two fine points. A screw action spaces the distance at which the two points are kept apart.

Drawplate: A steel plate with graded holes that can be round, triangular, D-shape, square, oval or rectangular. Annealed wire is drawn through the plate until the desired size and shape are achieved.

Electroplating: Means of transferring a thin coat of metal by the use of an electric current.

Enamelling: Fusing glass to metal at high temperatures.

Engraving: Cutting lines into, or removing areas from, metal with a sharp graver.

Etching: The use of acid to eat away exposed metal.

Facet: A flat polished surface on a gemstone.

File: A steel rod or thick sheet with "teeth" of varying sizes. Used for filing away metal. One stroke of the file cuts the metal, the reverse stroke does not.

Filigree: A decoration of fine wire, usually gold or silver and often twisted or plaited. The wire is often soldered to a sheet metal base; filigree without a base is called openwork. False filigree is an imitation formed by punching wire into the back of sheet metal or by casting from a true filigree original.

Findings: The means by which jewellery is secured – can be hooks, pins, butterfly catches, hinge joints.

Fire Stain: A blackish shadow which appears on silver, usually after polishing. It is the result of the copper in the silver mixing with the oxygen in the air during heating.

Flexible-shaft machine: A motor with a hand-held flexible drive shaft with a variety of tools used for drilling, texturing, polishing, etc.

Flux: A medium used to prevent oxidisation to allow solder to join the metal parts.

Foil: An ancient means of improving the colour and brilliance of stones by backing them with a thin leaf of highly polished metal.

Forging: Shaping metal with hammers by pushing and compressing it to the desired shape.

Former: A steel shape used as a support while shaping and forming metal.

Fusing: Joining metal together by melting the surfaces.

Gimp: Tiny piece of chenier squeezed together to hold the ends of nylon, tiger tail, or silk threads.

Girdle: The widest edge of a faceted stone.

Gold: A precious metal of bright yellow colour, well known for its ductility and malleability.

Granulation: Tiny silver/gold balls either soldered or fused to a metal surface for decoration.

Graver: Steel tool with sharpened, shaped point used for engraving.

Hallmark: Stamped marks on a piece of silver verifying the maker, the metal used, the office where it was assayed – or tested – and the year in which it was stamped.

Hyfin: A white polish used after Tripoli during the polishing process.

Investment: A fine plaster mixed with water and poured into a tube around a wax model before casting.

Jointing Tool: A hand tool used for holding chenier or rod, to help cut a straight line across it.

Lapis Lazuli: a complex mineral of an intense purple-blue, sometimes with inclusions of sparkling pyrites. Widely used for decoration and ornament, because of its colour and resistance to fading. The name possibly originated in the Middle Ages, "lapis" meaning stone and "lazuli" derived from the Arabic word for blue.

Lead Block: A malleable support for metal used in shaping.

Leather Pouch: Leather piece slung underneath the pin/workbench to catch metal filings.

Mallet: A wooden or rawhide hammer that is used like a hammer, but does not mark the former or the metal unless the metal is very soft.

Maltese Cross: A cross with four arms of equal length and size, which widen as they extend from the centre.

Mandrel: A tapered steel rod, hand held for tapping rings into shape.

Mica: Heat-resistant transparent sheet on which pieces to be enamelled are placed.

Micrometer: Hand tool which accurately measures the thickness of wire, sheet metal, drills, etc.

Mill: Set of stainless steel rollers used for reducing the thickness of metal.

Nickel Silver: A metal often used for costume jewellery.

Nitric Acid: Colourless acid which turns slightly blue when added to water and is used for "bright dipping" silver and for etching.

Oxides: Black or shadowy areas that appear when some metals are heated in air. Can be removed by pickling.

Pave Setting: Settings where stones are set flush with the metal and usually very close to each other.

Pickle: A solution, usually sulphuric acid and water, used after soldering and annealing to remove residual flux and oxides.

Piercing: Cutting out metal with a jeweller's or "piercing" saw which has very fine blades.

Pin: Wood block attached to a jeweller's bench used as a support.

Pitch: Mixture of Burgundy or Swedish pitch, plaster of Paris (or pumice powder) and tallow that supports work during chasing and repousse.

Planishing: Finishing the surface of metal with a highly polished planishing hammer. Planishing removes or flattens previous hammering marks.

Potassium Sulphide (Liver of Sulphur): Dissolved in water and used to deliberately oxidise a piece.

Pumice: An abrasive powder mixed with water used after pickling to clean the metal.

Quartz: A reference to its tendency to run across other mineral veins. The most common of minerals, it is mostly crystalline and come in three varieties plus many colours.

Repousse: Working a design into metal from the back.

Rivet: Method of joining – usually a small pin passing through two or more planes and spread out on both ends.

Rouge: A fine polish used after all other polishing has been completed. The powdered form is mixed with water and painted onto soldered joints to stop the solder from flowing in further heating.

Sandbag: A round leather pouch filled with sand used for shaping and supporting metal.

Scribe: Small pencil-like tool made from steel with a fine point used for marking out patterns on metal.

Shank: The body of a ring that fits around the finger.

Semi-precious Stones: A term generally used to refer to all gemstones other than the precious ones of diamond, ruby, emerald, sapphire and pearl.

Silver: Soft, white metallic element, very malleable.

Soldering: Joining one piece of metal to another by means of heat, flux, and solder.

Sprue: Rod attached to castings which forms a channel to the piece for the molten metal to flow down -after casting is complete, the sprue is cut away.

Stainless steel: Used for fine jewellery work.

Stoning: Rubbing enamels under water to a flat surface with a carborundum stone.

Sulphuric Acid: Colourless acid that becomes pale blue when in use. Used as a pickle for precious metals.

Swaging: Making U-shape from a flat piece of metal by placing it in a U-shape block and hammering it in with a former.

Tempering: Heating up the working end of a steel tool to soften it after it has been hardened.

Texture: An uneven surface given to metal to enhance its appearance.

Tiger's Eye: A term frequently used for decomposed Crocidolite, a fibrous mineral, ranging in colour from mauve to green.

Torch: Used for soldering, usually with a combination of gas and air.

Tripoli: A brown polish, usually used first in the polishing process.

Tweezers: (Brass): Used after heating metal to place it into and remove it from the pickle. (Insulated): Tweezers with insulated handles used for holding and placing pieces during soldering.

Ultrasonic: A cleaner which passes ultrasonic waves through the stainless steel container. It is used with an ammonia/detergent to clean polish from metal.

Work Hardening: When metal has been hammered, bent, or shaped until it becomes unmalleable. It should then be annealed.

INDEX